# HIJACKED
## *by Your*
# BRAIN

## How to Free Yourself When Stress Takes Over

### Dr. Julian Ford and Jon Wortmann

Published by Sourcebooks, Inc.
P.O. Box 4410, Naperville, Illinois 60567-4410
(630) 961-3900
Fax: (630) 961-2168
www.sourcebooks.com

Library of Congress Cataloging-in-Publication data is on file with the publisher.

Printed and bound in the United States of America.
VP 10 9 8 7 6 5 4 3 2 1

For Judy and Jen

# Contents

**Authors' Note**      **vii**

**Introduction**      **ix**

**Part I: Stress and the Brain**      **1**

Chapter 1: The Survival Brain      3

Chapter 2: The Learning Brain      21

Chapter 3: The Goal: Cultivate an Optimal Brain      41

**Part II: The Missing Step in Stress Management: Focusing**      **57**

Chapter 4: A Brief Introduction to SOS      59

Chapter 5: Step Back: Replacing Reactivity with Self-Regulation      69

Chapter 6: Orient: Regaining Your Inner Compass      77

Chapter 7: Self-Check: Reading Your Body's Dashboard      91

Chapter 8: When You Can't SOS: Recognize Triggers      109

**Part III: Three Ways to Orient before Stress Takes Over**      **125**

Chapter 9: Empower Your Emotions      127

Chapter 10: Exercise Your Core Values      143

Chapter 11: Determine Your Optimal Goals      159

**Part IV: An Optimal Life**      **171**

Chapter 12: Optimize Your Choices      173

Chapter 13: Make a Contribution      185

Chapter 14: Anticipating the Pitfalls on the Way to an Optimal Life      203

Appendix A: Further Reading                          213

Appendix B: A Summary of SOS                         217

Appendix C: A Summary of the FREEDOM Skills          221

Acknowledgments                                      223

About the Authors                                    224

# Authors' Note

Throughout the book, the stories we tell are true. We've had the privilege of seeing, and in some cases helping, thousands of people learn to regulate the stress alarm in their brains and take back control of their lives. In every case that we describe, the details of the story have been changed to ensure the privacy of each individual. Any resemblance in our writing to the people we've known or worked with is unintentional and should not be misinterpreted as a description of any specific individual. And, as you read our stories, we hope that you will see yourself in these people as they faced the ultimate challenge of modern life: transforming stress from a source of anxiety and despair into an opportunity to make the world a better place in which to live.

# Introduction

How do we stop stress from hijacking our lives?

No matter how well we handle stress, sooner or later it gets the best of us. No exceptions: even people who are incredibly calm and collected under intense pressure have stress meltdowns.

We work hard at managing stress, and still

- we find ourselves saying things we don't really mean during an argument
- we forget a promise we made to someone and have to deal with their disappointment and our guilt
- we back down instead of being assertive when confronted by a bully or abuser
- we get so revved up by competition that we can't think straight, or so nervous that we choke
- we act on impulse and do things that we know are wrong
- we find ourselves blaming someone else when we need to take responsibility
- we dwell on the past when we need to move on
- we feel unable to forgive ourselves or someone else
- we procrastinate or give up in the face of a crucial deadline
- we break down over the smallest thing

When stress takes over, and our better judgment and attempts to cope fail us, terrible things can happen, sometimes immediately, but often gradually. You don't notice until your life is in crisis, a relationship you deeply care about falls apart, or you wake up and realize you've lost track of how to be the person you know you can be.

But why does this happen? And what's the solution?

Scientists have begun a new line of research looking at how stress affects not just the body, but in particular the brain. Rather than focusing on our ordinary, day-to-day stressors, the research is conducted in a very specialized area known as *traumatic* stress or psychological trauma.

Traumatic stressors are the events that shock and terrify you, in which your life passes before your eyes. When they are over, you feel grateful to be alive. But the experience leaves a deep impact on the brain.

Research has not shown trauma to damage the brain; rather, trauma changes how the brain works. It also causes massive changes to how the body responds to stressful situations, and these changes can make the effort to cope with even the normal pressures of daily life feel overwhelming.

For many people, traumatic stressors result in something called post-traumatic stress disorder, or PTSD. PTSD can persist for months or years, but the research being done with patients has unlocked a way to help those whose stress reactions won't go away.

And *the emerging results from research on traumatic stress can help you too*, even if you haven't experienced trauma. What happens to the brain as a result of exposure to a traumatic stressor sheds new light on what's happening in the brain in every kind of stress meltdown.

It doesn't take a traumatic event to flood the body with stress hormones. It can happen when the phone just won't stop ringing. When a spouse or child does something annoying. When a driver cuts you off in traffic. When a coworker leaves you with a mess to clean up. It often happens for random reasons that don't seem to make sense.

Most of the time, you can handle the situation and effectively manage your own stress reactions. You take a deep breath, count to ten, remember not to sweat the small stuff, and move on. But then there are those times when stress reactions get out of control and spread like wildfire.

You see red: your blood pressure spikes, your heart pounds, and your mind races. You feel so stressed that you can't remember any of your stress management skills. You try to use a coping technique, but the stress reaction is so strong you can't calm down and your inability to relax makes you feel even worse.

An extreme stress reaction to an ordinary experience like bad traffic is not technically the same as the biological reaction to a life-threatening event, but the way the brain gets out of sync in both scenarios is remarkably similar.

*What do you do when you're too stressed to cope, and nothing you try seems to work?*

## The Missing Step: Listen to the Alarm in Your Brain

The answer is to listen to the alarm in your brain. Stress—or to be more precise, stress reactions—are not the problem. *They are a vital source of personal safety and health that need to be understood and valued.* That may sound completely crazy: how can a stress reaction possibly make life healthier? Hasn't stress been shown in scientific studies to cause countless illnesses and social problems? Doesn't stress make life miserable?

Yes and no. It's true that research has shown repeatedly that the more stressed a person feels—or the more a person's family, social, and work or school environments create the conditions that cause stress—the more likely they are to become ill or emotionally distressed. These studies, however, do not prove that stress reactions are harmful.

Stressful events trigger stress reactions, but there's a key missing link in this equation: stressful events trigger *a change in the brain*, which in turn triggers the body to have a stress reaction. That middle step is crucial. When we recognize the changes in our brains as they happen, instead of cascading into a meltdown, stress reactions become invaluable information that helps us create a happier, healthier life. The catch is you have to know your brain well to accurately translate the messages it sends.

To truly reduce stress, you have to understand the biology of your brain and how to use it to manage stress on your terms. What too many people have never been taught—despite more than a decade of groundbreaking scientific research—is that unmanaged stress reactions occur because there is *an alarm* in every person's brain. When triggered, this alarm can keep us safe from extreme danger and keep us focused in our day-to-day lives. When the brain's alarm becomes hyperactive, however, it can literally hijack the brain, your body, and your life.

In our attempts to find relief from the physical and emotional pain of extreme stress, we too often react without thinking and do things we later regret. Instead, we can learn to create a partnership between our brain's alarm and the centers of the brain that allow us to feel calm and in control. *Hijacked by Your Brain* has two purposes: to provide you with a user's guide to your brain, and to introduce you to skills that can change how your brain reacts to stress.

## The Science behind the Solutions

You have two guides on your journey through this book. As a clinical psychologist, Julian Ford has counseled hundreds of children, adolescents, and adults of all backgrounds suffering from traumatic stress and PTSD. His research and career have been dedicated to healing those who have survived profound violence, abuse, war, and natural disasters. For the past thirty-five years, he has worked with his colleagues and students to treat servicemen and servicewomen returning from combat, women and children living in poverty, adolescents and adults in the criminal justice system, and men and women in recovery from addiction and severe mental illness. Because of his emphasis on the core skill of emotional regulation, agencies including the World Health Organization, the National Institutes of Health, the U.S. Department of Health and Human Services, the Department of Veterans Affairs, and the Centers for Disease Control have sought his consultation on the treatment and prevention of traumatic stress.

Trained at Harvard in ministry, Jon Wortmann began his career in the public sector—working in hospitals and churches and with the homeless. When he began working with corporations on leadership development, he noticed that in every setting he visited, something was missing. Too often the solutions and support offered were reactions that stopped problems in the short term, but never taught individuals the skills to improve their situations. For Jon, discovering Julian's research was like Newton and his apple. Julian had found both the reason behind and the strategies to handle persistent patterns which adversely affect the health of both individuals and organizations. Jon tested Julian's methods with people who were sick or grieving, stressed-out executives, and even college athletes; every person reported an improved ability to manage stress.

We're writing this book together because, in our combined fifty years researching and caring for both those facing the worst traumas and regular people trying to deal with ordinary stressors, we've found a common problem: a misunderstanding of how the brain reacts to stress. Neither stress nor our brain is the enemy. There's nothing fundamentally broken or wrong with a brain that's having a stress meltdown. That brain is simply getting stuck in a prolonged and unnecessary stress reaction, and when we get stuck, we need a user's guide to help us break free.

## A User's Guide to Reducing Stress

We couldn't find a user's guide that explains how to unstick our minds and bodies when, or better yet, *before* a stress meltdown happens. We are fans of the many valuable books about how the brain functions, as well as those that teach techniques to manage stress, but there is a critical gap we want to address. Our goal is to help you understand how the brain changes under stress so you know how to use your brain with intention.

In part I, we'll explore the brain's stress reaction and stress management system. We'll show you how the brain can go into survival mode when the alarm is triggered, and how it naturally gravitates toward its thinking and memory centers that focus on learning. Instead of repeating the oft-made mistake of singling out stress as the problem, we'll show you how effective stress management actually involves using stress as an opportunity to create a partnership between the alarm and the brain's learning centers. When the brain's alarm and learning centers team up, the meltdowns stop happening, or become much briefer, milder, and more manageable.

Part II will show you how this partnership can be built and sustained in daily life by learning and practicing just two skills that are modeled on how the brain works most effectively. You might ask, "Doesn't it take antidepressant or anti-anxiety medications to balance the brain's chemistry, or even surgery?"

Medications can help, but they can't change how the brain's alarm system works. Medications can't activate the brain's learning system to partner with the alarm system. To do that, you need to teach the brain how to reset itself. And that means using the brain's greatest strength—the ability to think—in a way that creates a partnership between the different centers in the brain. Based in neuroscience, these two ways to focus in part II can be used to simplify rather than complicate the brain's role in stress reactions. The most efficient use of the brain is almost always the intentional act of focusing, and we'll explain how to focus in ways that are easy to remember and that have been proven effective in clinical trials.

In part III, you'll see that you already know many excellent ways to reset the brain's alarm, but these are almost always *not* the commonsense ways most of us have been taught to deal with stress. Even the experts on dealing with stress have placed too much emphasis on getting rid of, getting over, or rising above stress reactions. Stress reactions need to be used. They can't be eliminated and when they are caught early and viewed as offering useful information, they can help us learn to use our brains to focus on what is most important in our lives. We'll show you three powerful areas on which to focus your mind and body and overcome the common error of trying to silence or ignore the vital messages from your alarm.

When you know how to reset your brain's alarm using your brain's related systems for memory and thinking, you're back in control. Unfortunately, most of the people around you will still be trapped in the prison that misunderstanding stress and the brain can create. The final part will prepare you to use what you now know about how your brain works and then apply that learning in practical ways throughout the day, every day. You'll be ready to manage stress in your own life and to interact in a more meaningful way with the people who don't know what you have learned.

It is possible to prepare your brain to truly manage stress. And the result is well worth the effort: discovering a sense of calm and confidence that makes life ultimately worthwhile.

# Part I

## Stress and the Brain

# Chapter One

# The Survival Brain

Let's begin by introducing you to what stress feels like. Most of us know what extreme stress feels like, but often we don't notice the stress that is with us every moment of every day.

Check your stress level right now. On a scale of one to ten, ten being the most stressed you've ever felt and one being the most relaxed and happy you've ever been, where is your stress level right now?

If you're reading at home in a cozy chair, sitting on the beach during a vacation, or taking a break to have your favorite coffee, it ought to be quite low, maybe a one or a two. But if you're on a plane, and the person next to you is coughing, maybe your stress is at a three or a four. If you're surrounded by people you don't really like, or you're procrastinating and you've got a deadline, maybe it's even higher.

Now let's do a quick experiment.

Imagine all your money is gone. Worse, you're alone—no family and friends to help you—and you have nothing. Sit with that for a second.

Where is your stress level?

Did it go up from your initial self-check? For most people, just the idea of losing all their money will cause stress to rise. Each of us is capable of noticing what stress feels like, and throughout the book we will use the practice of measuring your stress level to help you to take control of stress rather than letting it take control of you.

Let's reduce your stress now.

Think of the person you love most, the person with whom you're totally comfortable. Imagine his or her face, happy and excited to see you. If you're with the person right now, just enjoy looking at him or her for a minute (if you're caught staring, just say you're doing an experiment, and you'll explain in a minute).

Did your stress go down?

Reducing stress depends on how completely you focus. If you could focus on the idea or experience of the person you love, your stress level probably went down. The fastest and best antidote for stress reactions usually is feeling secure in a primary relationship. If it didn't go down, that doesn't mean there's anything wrong with you. It simply means this wasn't the way for you to focus your thinking in this moment. Throughout the book we'll help you learn the best ways for you to manage stress by discovering what you want to focus on.

This initial experiment and the goal of chapter one is to make you aware of where stress comes from in your brain. Sometimes stress can come quickly and other times it's gradual. Noticing how your stress occurs helps you build the awareness you need to manage stress so you can experience life the way you do when you're at your best.

Unfortunately, that means we now need to raise your stress level again. Sorry for what we're about to do, but this is important.

Imagine you get this call: there's been an accident. The person you love most is in critical condition and is likely to die; you will never see the person again.

Feel the impact of that ugly thought for a few seconds.

Notice the thoughts and feelings that race through your mind and body. Notice how hard it is to think clearly, as if something were triggered in your brain and you can't even hear yourself think.

If you were willing to suspend your disbelief, you literally just felt your stress response rise.

Now imagine the person you love again.

Think about a favorite experience: something you love to do together, your favorite place for dinner, or the little thing the other person does that always makes you smile. If you can think about one experience where you feel completely loved, notice what happens. Feel your stress level fall.

Do you see how focusing your mind on what's most valuable and important to you in your life can change how you feel? We're not trying to toy with your emotions. Controlling stress comes from how, and on what, you choose to focus. Commonsense solutions we've been taught, techniques like thinking positively or solving problems, can be helpful. But before you can genuinely think positively or effectively solve a problem that's causing you stress, first you have to focus your mind on what's most important to you.

We're going to teach you how.

## The Irony of Stress and the Modern World

Learning how to focus our minds begins when we realize that our bodies are made to feel stress. It is part of our biological makeup to keep us safe and aware, but most days we treat this natural protective mechanism as a bad thing. We avoid the things that cause us stress unless—or until—we absolutely have to deal with them: we procrastinate at work or school; we wait until the last minute to have difficult conversations; we even leave our holiday shopping until the last possible day.

We try to ignore how we feel when we're stressed. We watch TV, play games on the Internet, or bury ourselves in a magazine or a novel. Unfortunately, when ignoring stress doesn't work, we try everything we can to feel better—even some things we know aren't good for us. And still, we can't escape stress.

*Stress is inevitable.*

To learn to manage stress effectively, you have to recognize that you can't avoid stress. In fact, it's natural to feel stress. The threats that cause our brains to produce stress are everywhere: rising prices, longer work-days than ever before, commutes that last hours, and homes underwater. Pressure is ubiquitous, and the complexity—over-scheduling, 24/7 connectivity, global competition—leaves us frazzled and weary. We're just so busy.

The irony, however, is that our modern lives also provide more access to resources and comfort—like information, food, climate control, indoor plumbing, health care, and entertainment—than at any point in human history. Yet none of these advances make us immune to stress.

Even more ironic is the proliferation of profoundly valuable stress management techniques. Most people in the twenty-first century know more about how to cope with stress than even the most powerful, privileged, or enlightened people of previous centuries.

Consider all the opportunities. Yoga is taught in most health clubs. Meditation groups meet at spiritual communities in every town. Insurance will pay for mindfulness training at most hospitals. Worship services are available in ancient traditions. We have fitness centers in most communities and myriad safe roads and trails for walking, running, and biking. Millions of mental health and human services professionals around the world offer counseling and scientifically proven therapies to ease everything from the pain of the worst traumas to the ordinary stress of work and family. And still, we too often feel stressed.

To take advantage of the resource that our brain can be for stress reduction, we have to know about the part of our brain that initiates stress reactions and how to use those reactions as helpful messages.

## The Alarm

*There is an alarm in every person's brain.*

Deep in an area that scientists believe is the source of all our emotions are two small almond-shaped regions called the amygdala. Found on both the left and right side of the brain, this ancient region of our central nervous system functions exactly like the clock alarm that wakes us up, and also like a fire alarm in a life-threatening emergency.

The amygdala's function is to signal the body whenever it's necessary to be alert. It sends two kinds of messages. Under ordinary circumstances, the first kind of message can be a normal shift from sleep to wakefulness. It is what happens when the body switches from daydreaming or boredom to paying attention. When a teacher or boss calls your name, it is the alarm that alerts your body and mind to refocus your attention and respond. The alarm also reacts when other people express needs or emotions, like a crying baby or a friend giving you that certain look or tone of voice that tells you they're annoyed. When you snap back to attention while driving when you weren't conscious of watching the road, it's your brain's alarm that sends you the wake-up call. Most of the time, the alarm in your brain is helpful, a kind of Jiminy Cricket, reminding you to focus your mind and attention when you need to.

You may never have noticed these gentle nudges from your alarm to be more alert, but you already know the difference between when your alarm is active and when it is quiet. The moment you wake up, the alarm usually operates at its lowest level, and your body feels calm and serene. On a typical morning, the alarm doesn't activate until you feel the shower's hot water or smell the coffee brewing. It raises your attention to little things like brushing your teeth so they stay healthy, or doing your morning yoga to stay strong and grounded. But then there are the mornings when you oversleep.

The jolt through your body when you sit up in bed and realize you're already late—that's the alarm in your brain too, only now it's adding a second message to the basic wake-up call. When you become aware of a problem—actually, well before you're consciously aware of it, when the deepest parts of the brain recognize a disconnect or looming trouble—the alarm sends a signal to take action. It says, "Don't just sit there, do something!"

It is the second kind of message, which comes with a surge of adrenaline, that feels like a jolt or intense distress. At that point, the alarm signals that you're facing an emergency, and that feels more like a blaring fire alarm than a gentle symphony from your bedside clock alarm. Your brain's alarm is no longer simply keeping you productively and enjoyably engaged in what you and the people around you are doing. Now, it's signaling the *red alert*. It's telling your body to mobilize all of its resources and deal with what the alarm perceives is an immediate crisis.

At this other extreme, the alarm serves a more serious purpose: namely, survival. When a person faces a threat or exposure to actual harm, the brain's alarm shifts into a state of heightened warning. This is the alarm's emergency function. A person who sees a man with a knife runs because the alarm sounds throughout the body. Someone who reacts without thinking and pushes another person out of the way of an oncoming car was capable of the heroic act because of the alarm. When there isn't time to stop and think because immediate action—fight or flight—is necessary to avoid, escape, or combat a threat to our lives, the alarm moves us to take action that can save us or someone around us.

## The Alarm Can Misfire

The problem with having this alarm in the brain is that certain types of stress can cause it to misfire. Anyone's amygdala can go from providing helpful reminders to wake up and be alert to becoming excessively reactive. Even more problematic is that the alarm can stay in *survival mode* even when there is no emergency, or when the crisis has passed and the problem has been solved. A great deal of the stress in our lives happens when the alarm mismatches the severity of its signaling with the actual level of danger.

For instance, let's say a salesman is late for a meeting. He runs out of the house without his car keys. When he dashes back in the door, his two-year-old daughter runs toward him and he screams, "Not now." His wife smiled when he walked in, thinking she would receive an extra kiss good-bye, but now she's ready to yell because his alarm reaction has triggered an equally strong reaction in *her* brain's alarm.

When the brain's alarm can't tell the difference between a survival threat and an ordinary life event, the default option appears to be for the alarm to signal a major emergency. For example, classic social psychology experiments from the 1950s and 1960s showed that ordinary people who were placed in situations that seemed to require extreme actions reacted by imposing unimaginably violent punishments on strangers and even fellow students. Even though they knew all along that they were in an experiment, they reacted in ways that were not what we would ordinarily expect.

In the famous Milgram Experiment, participants thought they were inflicting a hideously painful electric shock on a partner who was failing to meet the standards of the experimenter. The partners were actors, and the shocks weren't real, but the participants didn't know that. They kept delivering the shock, even though they thought they were truly hurting the other person, because the experimenter told them to. Each of them believed, "I have to do this!" The alarms in their brains overrode the clear choice they had to stop hurting the other person simply for answering a question incorrectly.

Each of them could have decided to do the right thing and stop what appeared to be incredible cruelty, but they weren't thinking clearly enough to remember their basic values. And that's not a criticism of them. This happens to each of us every day of our lives—it's just rarely this obvious and gut-wrenching when we make compromises to what really matters to us. We normally do it in smaller ways, like being nasty to our spouse or children when they make a small mistake.

In another study, the Stanford Prison Experiment, college students tasked with playing the role of prison guards became violently vindictive toward other students who were role-playing as prison inmates. These kinds of alarm-driven overreactions were not due to anything fundamentally bad or wrong with the participants, their values, or their brains. They were doing their best to deal with unexpectedly stressful challenges, and they didn't understand that their alarms perceived threat.

What went wrong was that their alarms were drastically misreading the seriousness of the problem, and triggered a *survival reaction* when it wasn't necessary. No one was really in danger, least of all the participants who inflicted the ill treatment. As Steven Pinker argued in *The Better Angels of Our Nature*, evidence is strong that we do not have an innate tendency toward cruelty. The best explanation of how these participants reacted then is that their brains sensed their survival depended upon extreme measures. When stress causes our brains to misread situations, it can lead to overreactions that cause harm in relationships, at work, or in any of the important parts of our lives.

*But how could a healthy brain do something as crazy as inflict cruelty on another human being when it wasn't truly necessary for survival?* When stress reactions build up over time, or after experiencing extreme stressors such as a traumatic accident, violence, or abuse, the brain's alarm can become overly sensitive and prone to overreact. We can be doing something as harmless as shooting baskets with our child, who accidentally hits us with the ball, and suddenly we find ourselves screaming at the child we love. In the studies, participants were not even conscious of this shift into survival mode in their feelings and thinking, but their actions tell the story. Most of us never recognize the onset of extreme stress until it's already too late, and we feel overwhelmed or ready to explode. But we can notice it sooner.

In the coming chapters we'll teach you how to turn down and reset your alarm, preventing both the perpetual feeling of being stressed and the extreme alarm reactions. Sometimes though, an extreme alarm reaction is necessary. There are times when we need the jolt of adrenaline and the physical, emotional, and mental power it provides to deal with one of life's true emergencies.

## The Hulk and Supermom

When Stan Lee and Jack Kirby created *The Incredible Hulk* in 1962, they exposed the comic's main character, Dr. Bruce Banner, to a deadly dose of radiation. In the original comic, the Hulk transformed from the buttoned-up, reserved doctor to his alter ego Hulk at sunset. The original comic was canceled after six issues, but the character wasn't finished.

While Lee cited Jekyll and Hyde and Frankenstein as his influences for creating the Hulk, Jack Kirby told the story of seeing a woman lift a car off her child. When the Hulk was brought back in issues of *Tales to Astonish*, he became the icon we know today. His transformation from scientist to giant green monster was caused by extreme emotional stress. Whether rooted in fear or anger, we can now say with playful certainty that the gamma radiation caused the Hulk to have the propensity for hyperactive alarm reactions.

And the comic book character raises a bigger question for our real-world understanding of our alarms. Whether Kirby really saw a mother lift a car off her child or the tale was effective media to promote the comic, is a mother really capable of lifting a vehicle off her child? The average weight of a car has changed through the years, but it generally hovers around 4,000 pounds. Can a human being really become like the Hulk?

The alarm fires on any occasion where there is a threat to us or to someone around us. At the extreme end of alarm reactions, there is no greater danger than a mother's child in life-threatening peril. Yet, can an extreme alarm reaction actually allow a person to lift twenty-five times her own body weight?

In 1982, Angela Cavallo, a woman in her late fifties, held up a 1964 Chevy Impala for five minutes while her son was rescued by neighbors. Reported by the Associated Press and confirmed by columnist Cecil Adams in an interview with Cavallo in 2006, her son was working on the suspension of the car in the family's driveway. He'd accidentally rocked the car off the jack, and when Angela came out of the house, she found him unconscious and pinned under the car.

According to Adams,

> *Hollering to the neighbor kid to get help, Angela grabbed the side of the car with both hands and pulled up with all her strength. The AP account said she raised the car four inches; she doubts it was that much but believes*

*it was enough to take the pressure off. She recalls nothing about the rescue,*
*but the AP said two neighbors reinserted the jack and dragged the boy out.*

Her son recovered completely. The question is: could a five-foot-eight woman really pull off a feat normally reserved for strongest man competitions? This is within the range of possibility in terms of what the brain's alarm makes possible through our bodies. The story illustrates an important point we don't want you to forget: the alarms in our brains are not the problem—often, in fact, they're the source of solutions. We need the alarm under extreme circumstances to give us the chance to survive or help someone else live. Firefighters would never enter a burning building if they did not have such an alarm. A mother would never catch her child before she falls off a chair if she did not have an alarm looking for potential threats to her health and the safety of those she loves.

The problem with stress is that most of us *don't know how to turn our brains' alarms down when it is stuck in the "on" position.* Remember your initial self-check level, with one being completely without stress and ten being extremely stressed. Too often we stay at a level seven or eight, when we could easily be at a one, two, or three, relaxed and focused on what's most important in the moment. Instead, long after the emergency is over and we no longer need our alarm to keep us alert or get us out of trouble, we still react with the same intensity to experiences that aren't urgent or life-threatening.

## The Two Types of Stress Reactions

Recognizing the signals, both when the brain's alarm is active and when it is turned down, begins with understanding the physical sensations an alarm or stress reaction creates in our bodies. The moment the brain senses trouble, the alarm activates the body's stress response system. When our ancient ancestors hunted and gathered to stay alive, their brains had to keep them on guard against constant hazards. The world was wilder. Danger lurked, and their brains perpetually focused on keeping them safe.

We're not going to run into a lion at the grocery store, but despite the evolution of our species, our brains still scan every situation for trouble. The problem most of us face in the modern world is that the stimuli that bombard us cause our brains to think we're in trouble all the time. When things have gone poorly at work and our phone buzzes in our pockets, we worry it's our boss or someone calling with bad news. To the brain, when our alarms are hyperactive, the buzzing phone can be the same experience as seeing a hungry lion. Remembering, in the middle of the night, the email we promised we'd send can produce the same feeling of panic as seeing our child under a car.

When the brain senses trouble, the alarm sends a stress alert through the nervous system so the body is primed to protect itself. Normal stress reactions include

- tensing up
- elevated heart rate
- feeling agitated or exhilarated
- sweating
- breathing heavily
- shaking

These physical stress reactions are the body's way of preparing to meet a challenge. That's why they're called the *fight or flight* response; they mobilize the body's physical resources to either fight back against an enemy or escape to avoid harm. They often are called an adrenaline rush because the brain's alarm signals the adrenal gland to produce and circulate adrenaline along with other stress chemicals. While adrenaline prepares the body to defend itself against a potential danger, it's the last thing you want when you're trying to relax and enjoy dinner with your family.

The other type of stress reaction that the brain's alarm can trigger takes almost the opposite form. Sometimes when the body becomes flooded with adrenaline, instead of gaining superhuman strength, we shut down. This *freeze* stress reaction occurs when the body's nervous system slams on the brakes as a way of preparing to cope with a potential threat. Like animals that stay still to prevent detection, the alarm reacts. Its reactions don't make sense until we consider that it is simply the ancient part of the brain trying to keep us safe.

The freeze reaction is not better or worse than the fight or flight response. Instead of experiencing the adrenaline rush that causes us to feel agitated, anxious, or angry, we feel exhausted, too tired to fight back or escape. In the short run, freezing may be highly adaptive, for example when you need to stop and scope out a potentially dangerous situation. But when you can't *un*freeze, you can feel paralyzed. You can end up not just pausing but *shutting down*. That's when freezing can feel like falling apart, like you're too exhausted to run or defend yourself, even when you really want to.

Both stress reactions can be helpful or harmful depending on the emergency. The important point is that what we feel when we're stressed can take several forms, which look very different on the surface, but share a common source: a signal from the brain's alarm. When we recognize we're having a stress reaction, that's when we can do something about it.

## The Worst Drive in Masters History

When Rory McIlroy stood on the 13th tee, he slumped, his head buried in his elbow. His chance to do what no other Irishman had ever done was over. One of the top-rated golfers in the world, McIlroy began the final round of the 2011 Masters golf tournament in Augusta, Georgia, with a four-stroke lead.

In golf, the Masters is one of, if not the most, coveted championships. It is an invitational event on a course designed by one of the game's greats—Bobby Jones. The players who have won are familiar even to non-golfers: names like Tiger Woods, Jack Nicklaus, and Arnold Palmer. The story of McIlroy's epic fail that day is actually a story about the brain's alarm and what happens to it in moments of great stress, perceived or real. It's also a story with a happy ending.

McIlroy made the turn to the final nine holes of the tournament before five o'clock. The weather was ideal. He held a one-shot lead as he hit his tee-shot on the 10th hole. At 4:53, what had already been a stressful day of trying to maintain the lead headed toward disaster. His drive, normally the strength of his game, went so far left the TV cameras couldn't find it. His normal drives travel 300 yards; this one went 100 yards and ended up between two cabins. The commentators on television had never seen a shot so wild, particularly from a man leading the tournament. Even after such a wayward shot, he was still in the lead.

But not for long.

When the alarm creates a survival reaction, even the best athletes can't think straight or do what they've done naturally thousands of times before. Coaches have been telling players for years to have a positive attitude and to look like a winner. What most have not explained to their students is why sometimes even the best athletes struggle to remain confident.

After punching out into the fairway, McIlroy ultimately took five shots to get to the green. He would miss the putt and take a seven on the hole. His seven, a triple bogey, meant he was two shots behind three other players. But that was only the beginning of the fall.

He three-putted the next hole, something professionals rarely do, after a reasonable chance at birdie (one shot under par). He then four-putt for double-bogey on the 12th hole, something that professionals may do only one time in a tournament in an entire year.

What happened to Rory McIlroy is a perfect example of an alarm out of control. He described the meltdown in his post-round press conference.

> *I thought I hung in pretty well in the front nine. I was leading the tourna-*
> *ment going into the back nine, just hit a poor tee shot on 10 and sort of*
> *unraveled from there. Just sort of lost it 10, 11, 12, and couldn't really*
> *get it back. It's one of those things; I'm very disappointed at the minute*

*and I'm sure I will be for the next few days, but I'll get over it. I have to take the positives and the positives are I led this golf tournament for 63 holes. I'll have plenty more chances; I know that. It's very disappointing what happened today and hopefully it will build a little bit of character in me as well.*

The stress he felt at the beginning of the day was not brought on by a real threat to his safety. He was not at war. There was no lion chasing him. His brain perceived a great danger in what was at stake and his body reacted. As he struggled to feel comfortable on the golf course, the weight of what he wanted to accomplish—win for his career and country, become one of the greats in history by winning the event, earn over a million dollars and millions more in endorsements—caused his alarm to become hyperactive. He tried valiantly to stay calm and focused, but he couldn't *because he didn't know how to reset his brain as it took over his body.*

When he hit the wayward drive, with an alarm that may already have been at a six, seven, or eight, his brain kept pumping adrenaline. His thoughts swirled with what his failure would mean, his muscles tightened, and his chances of winning were over. Although he would recover and play respectably the last three holes, instead of winning the coveted title, his inability to control his alarm caused him to finish in a tie for 15th place.

Some golfers who have crumbled under the pressure of trying to win have never returned to their former level of play or have given up the game completely. But notice again what McIlroy said at the press conference just moments after his disappointment. After admitting his frustration, he said, "I'll have plenty more chances; I know that."

The same young man who stood slumped over a few hours previous, completely unable to control his alarm, sat in front of a press corps. They were drooling for the young phenom to make an equally compelling mess out of his post-round comments.

Instead of crumbling, he was confident. He was calm. He had already recovered his composure and in just as difficult a task—golf and public speaking are both deeply affected by alarm reactions—he succeeded in connecting with the world. He had, in fact, turned down his alarm. And a few months later, he got the chance to control his alarm again on another of golf's biggest stages.

At the U.S. Open, which like the Masters is one of golf's four major tournaments coveted by every player, McIlroy once again held a commanding lead going into the final round. He said in his interview the evening before the final eighteen holes, "From the experience I had at Augusta, I know now how to approach tomorrow, and I think that's the most important thing…The more I put myself in this position, the more and more comfortable I'm becoming."

He had learned to manage his alarm under what for a golfer is the most stressful moment in a career. McIlroy would win the tournament by eight strokes, setting the record for the lowest score in U.S. Open history. What he learned to do intuitively, you can learn to do as well—and maybe without having to make such a painful mistake.

## You Can't Turn Off the Alarm, and You Wouldn't Want To

If you didn't have an alarm, you'd always be late. You'd live in a cloud of meaningless time with nothing more important than anything else. You'd never care about people. Our alarms call us to pay attention to the real needs in relationships, and while at times most of us go too far with our alarm reactions, the instinct is still what makes us human. Before we teach you the parts of the brain that can set you free from stress, it is essential to explore what most of us do wrong.

Instead of learning to use stress as a teacher, we hide from it. The millennia-old methods of stopping or numbing the alarm are as familiar to us as stress itself.

- We deny our alarms—"Nothing is wrong; I should just relax and stop overreacting."
- We self-medicate with alcohol, other drugs, eating, shopping, sex, and overworking, to name just a few of human beings' favorite numbing techniques.
- We blame ourselves or the people around us for the normal feelings that come from an alarm which just wants to keep us alert and safe. We say, "It's all my fault" or "It's all their fault."

Why don't we think of bodily or emotional stress reactions as an opportunity? Whether we use denial, self-medication, or blame, in each case we fail to take the alarm's message seriously. These alarm reactions often seem like more of a problem than any of the real problems that the alarm calls for us to deal with. That's when we make the mistake of trying to shoot the messenger. We just want to make the brain's alarm stop going off.

We can't turn the alarm off, and we don't actually want to. Without an alarm, in addition to getting seriously hurt because we couldn't prevent life-threatening emergencies, we wouldn't be able to perform at our best. The essence of peak experience—living the life you want on your terms—is the ability to channel our focus. That comes from the alarm first making you aware that focusing is important. We can each, if we want to, learn how to channel the alarm's messages into a way of living where our biggest challenges can be overcome and our dreams become possible.

## The Survival Brain in Everyday Life and on a Global Scale

In trying to manage our stress, the ongoing problem for all of us comes down to this question: how do we turn down our alarms when the world is more stressful than ever?

New studies about work and family life reveal that 37.8 percent of professional men and 14.4 percent of women are now working more than fifty hours per week. That's millions of hours in every country on earth that used to be spent on leisure now poured into the inherently more stressful environment of work.

Recent research on working parents found that working mothers spend 10.5 more hours per week than working fathers multitasking while at home. A curious finding from researchers at Bar-Ilan University in Israel and Michigan State University in the United States, including 368 mothers and 241 fathers, was that mothers report their multitasking to be stressful, while fathers report it to be rewarding.

Why? What's going on with the mother's alarm that's not happening for Dad's? It may be the greater responsibility that mothers tend to take for family and home rather than a gender difference that explains the divide in resilience to stress. Fathers may under-report the stressfulness of multitasking—minimizing or ignoring alarm signals because the last thing they want to feel at home is more stress. What we know for sure when considering modern work and home life is that we're all busier, multitasking more, and prone to more hyperactive stress reactions.

Scholars in every field are trying to discover the impact of doing too much because most of us are continuously paying attention to too many things, hoping our bodies and brains can take the stress. The reality from the perspective of our alarms is clear: we can handle incredible amounts of stress, until we can't. And these days, the whole world and almost everyone in it seems to be having a prolonged alarm reaction.

The financial crisis that began in 2008 put entire countries in a heightened alarm state. Banks did not lend to customers who in the past would have been highly qualified out of fear of more losses. This illustrates stress reactions on a mass scale: bankers and the entire global financial system in survival mode with their brains' alarms ramped up by the near-catastrophic excesses of the past decade. With not just banks but entire countries on the brink of financial default, it's inevitable that the brains of bankers (and politicians) produced and continue to cause intense survival reactions.

The result is a worsening of an already precarious situation. This survival reaction means that banks don't provide prospective homeowners the funds they need to buy the homes that current homeowners need to sell, contributing to the crisis of foreclosures. When banks then fail to lend to employers who need money to be able to hire and keep their workforce, unemployment can't improve. It's not a matter of money; the problem is that the entire financial system is in crisis because too few people in it know how to recognize, understand, and deal with the extreme survival reactions in their brains.

So what do we do when stress derails our lives? Free our brains. The best news about our alarms is that while they seize control when they sense danger, the brain also has incredibly powerful internal resources to turn the alarm down, and in fact, reset the stress response. Our survival brain is a powerful tool to keep us alert and safe; we possess an even more powerful tool that can make every part of modern life feel better. It's the part of us that creates the feeling of calm and confidence: the learning brain.

# Chapter Two

# The Learning Brain

We opened chapter one by having you measure your stress. The purpose was to introduce you to what it feels like when your alarm is on, either trying to make you alert or keep you safe. Now imagine the low-stress situations again: quietly reading, sitting on the beach, or enjoying that great coffee.

On a different scale of one to ten, where one means that you have no control in your life because you're totally confused or acting without thinking, and ten means that you're in absolute control because you're thinking with complete clarity about whatever is most important to you in your life, *where is your personal control level right now?*

In addition to measuring the stress reactions from your brain's alarm system, you can measure the sense of personal control that your brain can produce. The *opposite* of stress is not total relaxation or sleep, but the active feeling of being in control. Personal control can take the form of feeling calm and pleasantly energized. It's what you experience when you're deeply interested in something that you enjoy. But being in control is not just a feeling. It is a very specific ability.

Personal control is your capacity to *think so clearly* that you make the most of whatever happens right now. Personal control is not measured by physical strength, financial wealth, or social popularity. People who are truly in control of their lives can't dictate exactly what happens or how everything works out, but they can think in a way that allows them to effectively handle whatever life throws at them. What is your level of personal control, your ability to think clearly, right now?

Because we primed you with low-stress images and because you're reading (generally a low-stress activity), it's likely that you feel a high level of personal control at this moment, maybe a six or seven, or even a ten. You're choosing to enjoy this book and because you're learning, you're thinking with a high level of clarity. A ten, thinking with total clarity, is rare, but if you're totally focused right now, it's possible.

When shocking, frustrating, or miserable things happen, however, we all tend to feel stressed. Along with the stress, we often feel so confused or emotionally amped up or shut down—remember both are normal stress reactions—that thinking clearly becomes difficult. That lingering feeling that things are not right, which can become a nagging frustration or worry, that's the brain's alarm too. And any time our brains are alarmed, our reduced ability to think clearly reduces our sense of personal control.

*No matter how smart and capable you are under ordinary circumstances, when you have a major stress reaction your sense of personal control may drop drastically, precisely because you're not thinking clearly.*

That's not news, but what is new to most of us is the fact that feeling stress doesn't mean there is something wrong with us. Feeling out of control almost always is the result of not being able to think clearly, not of a deeper or more serious problem. But when we feel out of control, we can get angry, scared, impulsive, and even desperate. That's the real problem: feeling helpless can cause the brain's alarm to overreact, and this leads to out-of-control actions.

There's a good reason too. At times of high stress, the brain's alarm takes over the brain's thinking center. The alarm in survival mode literally hijacks the brain, and along with it, your ability to think clearly and choose the path of your life. But it takes over to try to keep you alive, not to torture or harm you. And it needs the help of the rest of your brain, desperately, in order not to become so reactive that it actually creates more problems than it prevents.

# How to Soothe Your Inner Two-Year-Old

To deepen your awareness of the challenge of managing stress, here's a comparison that's hard to forget: your brain's alarm is like a two-year-old who feels insecure.

The alarm isn't interested in learning. It has one job: to keep you alert, aware, and alive. Anything else—like enjoying life, building good relationships, achieving personal goals—means nothing to it. It does not understand logic, so you can't reason or argue with it. The smallest things can set it off, and when distressed it can make a big fuss for a long time. The only way to calm down your brain in the middle of a survival reaction is to give it what it wants.

We might think a two-year-old only wants to play and eat sweets. But actually, what young children want most is to see that the adults who offer them security (like parents) are paying attention to them when *they* want attention from the adult. Mostly two-year-olds want to be left alone to do whatever they find most interesting. But when they feel insecure, they want to know *their* adult security is there for them—right away, without any delay, totally focused on them and nothing else. Helping any two-year-old recover when they feel extremely upset involves calmly communicating reassurance that everything is going to be all right because you know how to help the child get what he or she wants.

Evidence that you know how to handle a challenge and everything *really* is going to be all right is what shifts the brain's alarm from being stuck in survival mode to the calm place where you can focus on what really matters to you. This is the true challenge of stress management: *how do you reassure, soothe, and reset an area in the brain that you can't see or talk to?*

When managing stress, in fact, what most people do actually turns *up* the alarm. Most of us have spent our whole lives trying to identify, prevent, or correct problems, ranging from the trivial to the life-threatening. We've been living in survival mode because we've been taught that's how you get ahead and achieve success. But such striving induces stress. When we then tell ourselves to "relax," it doesn't work because the command tells the alarm there really is something to get stressed about. When we say to ourselves, "get over it," "don't be so upset," or "don't worry," the alarm only sounds louder because our declarations actually send the signal that we can't handle the current stressor.

The alarm will only stop the flow of stress chemicals and give control of our body back to the learning brain when it knows that we're safe or that we can handle any danger or problem, even if it can't be completely resolved or eliminated. The more we say, "stop being a complainer," the more the alarm perceives that we're in real danger. If we tell ourselves to "grow up," the alarm will continue to ratchet up our stress response.

*The alarm can't tell the difference between real danger and perceived danger.* You can't tell a toddler who is crying for no reason to "stop crying." You turn her attention to her favorite toy or you pick her up. If an experience has caused us stress before, just saying everything is better isn't evidence for the alarm that the trouble has passed. The alarm needs the learning brain to focus on an experience that actually is better than whatever causes the feeling of stress.

Your brain has a survival system designed to protect you, but it can also accelerate out of control, and we hope you're beginning to see why you feel stress on a regular basis. You also have had many experiences where you feel in control, even in the middle of a stressful life. Your brain already has pathways ready to keep you calm and thinking clearly. You are not only equipped to survive, your brain is also hardwired to explore the world and learn.

## The Two Key Parts of the Learning Brain

We are all capable of thinking clearly because we have learning brains. The learning brain, which is the biological source of what we think of as our rational mind, is coordinated by two regions called the prefrontal cortex and the hippocampus.

The prefrontal cortex, the brain's *thinking center*, is located in the very outer layer of the brain closest to the skull, and right behind the forehead.

It is responsible for translating everything we sense, perceive, and feel into intelligent thoughts. That includes being able to put what you experience with your five senses, and what you feel emotionally, as well as what you think, into words.

The prefrontal cortex is the brain's thinking center because it takes what we experience in life and turns it into *learning*. And not just any kind of learning: we're not talking about simply developing a habit or a way to do something physical (like driving a car, playing a musical instrument, or excelling at a sport). Those are important kinds of learning, but not what makes life most interesting. In addition to our habits and the skills we rely on, what makes life fulfilling is the ability to know how all of our actions, abilities, and experiences add up to something bigger than any single talent or accomplishment.

*The unique facility of the thinking center is to think about what life means.* It helps us decide what's most important to us. This may seem like a luxury, but focusing on what's most important is, according to Julian and his colleagues' research with those recovering from the worst kinds of psychological trauma, essential for all of us.

We all ask ourselves countless times, why am I doing this? What's the point? And we then make the mistake of thinking that this is just an idle question, a foolish way of contemplating our navels. In truth, meaning is what our brains *always* think about—except when we're in survival mode and the alarm takes over.

You know when your thinking center is really working. You're aware that somehow what you're doing right at that moment is totally worthwhile. You may not be consciously considering a particular deep question or desire, but still you have a sense that what's happening right now matters. It feels important because you're engaging in something that you believe in. That could be something as simple as keeping your house neat or as complex as having a deep and reflective conversation about your goals in life.

When you focus on something that is truly important to you, you're activating the thinking center in a way that goes beyond practical problem solving or simply expressing your thoughts: you're tapping into a key hidden ability of the brain. When it's operating effectively, the prefrontal cortex signals your alarm that you have things under control. Your thinking center soothes your inner toddler because it sends the unmistakable message that you recognize and know how to handle whatever is causing your alarm to feel worried or upset. *The capacity to intentionally focus on what's most important is the missing step that few of us have been taught when trying to manage stress.*

And soothing the alarm also involves another, just as vital, part of your mind. The hippocampus, the brain's memory filing and retrieval center (or *memory center* for short), is located much deeper in the brain—in fact, right next to the amygdala (the alarm). The hippocampus is like the brain's librarian, filing every experience we have as a memory.

The entire brain is a storehouse for memories, but it is the memory center (often with some help from the alarm, especially when memories have a strong emotional charge) that collects and places each memory in the brain—like a team of librarians deciding where to file books on the shelves. Some memories are like bestsellers and get stored in a way that is quick and easy to find, while others get buried deep in our brains for the rare occasion we'll use the information.

Memories take many forms. Our memories include feelings, ideas, images that we've seen, visual replays of what we've done and what's happened to us, sounds that we've heard, and even the subconscious cues that keep us safe. Some memories are complicated; they tend to be organized, like stories in a book or movies and TV shows. Other memories are simpler and more scattered, like a collection of mementos put in a box in the attic for safekeeping.

It's an immense and complex system, but it's important to appreciate how your brain works so you can take advantage of its power to handle stress reactions by thinking clearly. When the hippocampus goes to retrieve a memory, it may end up with a complicated combination of all of these forms of memory. It doesn't usually just get a simple executive summary—like, "I went to the store and bought some milk." Instead, it gets a blow-by-blow description of everything that happened: how we felt and what we were thinking; what we saw and heard that left the most lasting impression; how we feel and what we think now when we recall the memory.

The elegant complexity reaches another level when we reflect on how different parts of the brain search for and deal with memories. It's not just the thinking center in the brain that puts in requests for memories. The alarm also asks for what we remember; but, in keeping with its relatively immature and emotional nature, these requests usually are more like demands or commands. Where the thinking center might say, "I'm interested in recollecting what I learned from past experiences that can help me make a good choice in this present moment," the alarm might scream, "I *need* to remember every possible bad experience that can help me survive this present experience, and *right now!*"

When the thinking center requests a relevant memory, the memory center can take its time and check carefully to find the most helpful files. Memories can come to us quickly, but they don't have to. The thinking center doesn't work on deadlines because it's trying to learn, not urgently solve a problem.

When the alarm demands a memory, however, the memory center tends to react like anyone would when put under tremendous pressure: panicking and rushing to grab the first memory it can find, even if it's not the right one. That's why, when under extreme stress (or when feeling extremely stressed even if there really isn't a big problem), we tend to feel emotionally confused and overwhelmed, and to think in an equally confused and ineffective way.

When the hippocampus is working effectively, it files new memories in a way that makes them easily and accurately retrievable, and it can actually retrieve the correct memory efficiently—like finding the right file in a computer system's list of folders with a simple search. Memories that we need on a regular basis go into our *daily* files, and those that we'll only need occasionally go into our *once in a blue moon* files. The memories that are most easily filed and retrieved in each category are those that have a strong emotion attached to them. New research reveals this is probably because the amygdala (which handles the emotion) and the hippocampus (which handles the factual information) team up to file those memories.

When the amygdala is out of control, however, reacting to extreme traumatic stressors or to persistent ongoing stresses, the hippocampus rapidly becomes overloaded and breaks down. Our alarms can literally cause us to misfile memories. A terrible trauma that should go into the blue moon file, like being physically abused or nearly dying in a *head-on* automobile crash, may be filed as something that is about to happen again at any moment every day. That's a big part of what's wrong when a person develops post-traumatic stress disorder. In the chaos and confusion, memories get filed automatically in the section of information we need daily—like how to brush our teeth—when they belong in the section of the memory center that's only accessed occasionally.

For instance, a memory of an experience in which we coped well with a problem that wasn't possible to completely solve, like a complicated family argument, might be misfiled as a result of an alarm reaction. The alarm views that experience as a disaster or a total failure. When we face a similar challenge in the future, instead of remembering how well we handled a difficult situation, the memory center retrieves a feeling of anxiety, frustration, or depression, often accompanied by a blast of self-doubt. Recalling the misfiled memory amps up the alarm even more, leading to the feeling that stress never gets better. Our brains, having misfiled the memory, continually escalate our stress, causing us to feel totally out of control.

Scientific research with people who have experienced traumatic stressors and are suffering from PTSD has shown that remembering the traumatic events leads the brain's alarm to become hyperactive. At the same time, the thinking center and the memory center seem to shut down or go off-line. The alarm cries out for attention and help, but the more that it does, the worse the updates to the memory center become. This leads the memory center to retrieve painful rather than helpful memories. The thinking center then becomes incapacitated by the combination of the screaming alarm and the overwhelming memories.

Fortunately, most of us don't have PTSD and therefore don't have alarm reactions quite this extreme most of the time. But even someone who has never experienced trauma can have an alarm meltdown that is just as severe. We all have an alarm that can go into a state of panic or rage, and most of us don't know how to use our thinking centers to pay attention to the alarm regularly and in a way that makes its messages valuable.

The good news, maybe even the best news no one has ever taught you, is that it is entirely possible to use the prefrontal cortex to help the hippocampus select memories in a very different way than usual—a way that results in clearer thinking. Clear thinking resets the alarm to a lower level. This is what we all want when feeling stressed: to be able to switch our attention from false or unhelpful perceptions of danger to thoughts and memories that enable us to regain a sense of calm and personal control.

Though it does not come naturally to most of us, we can adjust our stress reactions by using the brain's thinking and memory centers in a highly focused way. By focusing the thinking center on how we've got the situation handled, even if there is actually some danger involved, the memory center can pull up helpful memories. Knowing how to focus turns down the alarm and ultimately resets it. This is what creates confidence, and during the best successes of your life, you've learned to do this intuitively.

## Stage Fright

Woody Allen began his career as a nineteen-year-old, writing comedy for television programs like *The Ed Sullivan Show* and *The Tonight Show*.

But in 1961, his managers Jack Rollins and Charles Joffe decided that he could be an entertainer. While Allen saw himself as a writer, Jack Rollins convinced him to try stand-up comedy. Allen remembers what Rollins said. "Do me a favor, just trust me. You just work, and don't think about it. And let me think about it. Do what I tell you, and let's look up in a year and see where you are."

For a year, he was a failure. His material was funny and his presence—as a small, cerebral man with thick glasses and a deliberative way of speaking—earned a few laughs; but mostly, audiences didn't understand his style. Rollins kept telling friends and colleagues that Allen was "unique," and that he was an "industry." Allen had a terrible time. He was shy. He had to be pushed on stage. He threw up before performances.

Stage fright is completely normal, and fully understandable when we consider our brains' alarms. Going out in front of a crowd to talk, sing, or dance, the performer risks everything. Laurence Olivier was an eager performer in his youth, but as he got older, like Allen, he too had to be pushed before the lights. Rod Stewart, the famous pop rock singer who has sold over one hundred million records, once sang an entire song from behind speakers. Barbra Streisand forgot the lyrics to one of her songs during a concert in Central Park in 1967 and didn't perform again live for over thirty years. Allen was having the same kind of stress response that plagues most entertainers at one point or another in their careers.

Then one night, it changed. Allen went on stage, did the same routine, and was an entirely different person. His friends saw the persona we know today from so many television and movie performances. He was quick, vibrant, and immersed in enjoying his own jokes. He was figuring out how to get the reaction that would be most interesting to him, rather than figuring out what he had to do so the audience wouldn't hate him. His six-week run at The Bitter End in Greenwich Village, New York, earned raves from critics, and by 1962, catapulted him to the heights of the stand-up world.

So what happened? How does a meek, overly thoughtful writer who can't bear the spotlight suddenly become his best self in front of a critical New York City crowd? Quite simply, his brain switched from surviving to learning. He went from the bashful, careful performer who didn't want to fail to the calm, confident comedian who was exploring how to make people laugh. It's possible to make this transition. It's not a mysterious secret either. You don't have to go through thirty years of exile, and while it helps to have teammates who will give you a push, every human being is capable of making the transition Woody Allen did.

## Remove the Have-To's

How do you reset a primitive system in the brain that is in survival mode? First, get rid of the have-to's. If you're like most of us, you spend too much of your day lost in a flood of less important thoughts about what's frustrating, pressuring, or worrisome. Notice that we didn't advise you to simply think positive or reassuring thoughts. Nor did we suggest that you try to figure out everything about the current situation and come up with a comprehensive solution or plan of action. We also didn't tell you to just take some deep breaths and relax.

None of this will activate your thinking center so it can reassure, and turn down, your brain's alarm. Positive thinking, deep, calming breaths, and relaxing are the *result* of your alarm getting its needs met, not the way to give the alarm what it wants or needs. When your brain's alarm gets the attention it wants, it goes back to being calm and leaves you to do whatever you need to do. You know what it feels like when this happens: your body relaxes, feels less stressed, and you can think clearly again.

What you probably didn't know is that you're not feeling better because you took some deep breaths or thought some positive thoughts or solved a problem. You're feeling better because you, using your learning brain, chose to pay attention to your brain's alarm. *Then* you could take a deep breath and enjoy what you're doing. Then you could think positive thoughts because you're actually feeling positive. Then you could solve a problem because you could think clearly again.

We all tend to get this in the wrong order. We think that first we'll relax and fix problems, and then we'll feel less stressed. But the truth is when we pay attention to the needs of our alarms first, then we can relax and solve problems.

Most of the time we run around doing what we have to do. We're inviting you to stop that method of thinking and living. You don't have to make everyone else happy. You don't have to solve every problem at work. You don't have to make your children the next president or superstar.

Remember, the brain's alarm is designed to keep us alive when necessary—but it's much better at keeping us alert and aware *if* it's not operating in the red zone at a stress level of nine or ten. Resetting the alarm is the key to maintaining a low stress level, where it can do its job by keeping us focused instead of making us more stressed and miserable.

Understanding the brain's alarm gives you the key to solving this problem. You begin to reset the alarm in your brain simply by paying attention to it, not by trying to avoid or ignore it.

## The Talent Show

The transition from living with a highly active or hyperactive alarm to a focused, calm, and confident mind can often feel like waking from a dream. When Mary Beth came to see us, all she wanted to do was sing in her high school's talent show. At fifteen years old, she was good; she had the kind of naturally gifted voice grandparents and friends commented on when she sang casually around the house. She took voice lessons and had belonged to school choirs since elementary grades. She watched shows like *American Idol* and practiced in front of the mirror for imaginary auditions.

When she came for help though, it wasn't for an audition to get on TV. Her school had an annual talent show, and she just wanted to try out. But she didn't think she could. The thought of standing in front of a few upper classmen and a couple of teachers caused her to freeze. She turned strawberry red; she couldn't get a single note out. As we worked her through the first skill in stress management (which we'll introduce in part two), she relaxed. Her nervousness didn't disappear, but now she had a high level of personal control even when her alarm was elevated.

We had her practice in front of her parents. Then we asked her to bring in a few friends. In a few weeks, she was singing her heart out at a small event, but it wasn't the talent show. In our final sessions we didn't talk about Mary Beth's fear of performing, but rather where she wanted to take her singing and how she wanted to help other kids get over their fears. A few days before the audition, when we asked what she was thinking about, she said, "I'm still really nervous, but now I know that's not a bad thing."

Then the day of the audition, it snowed. School was canceled, and that morning she called, crying. She could barely talk. When we asked her what was wrong, she said, "Nothing." As she gathered herself, she said, "I'm crying because I'm so happy! Last night I couldn't have been more nervous. Even though I thought I was better and I did everything we talked about, I still felt sick to my stomach. I barely slept. Then, when school was canceled, it all went away. I had to call you because now I realize I was nervous for nothing. The nerves aren't going to stop me and now I realize I can keep trying to sing. No matter what happens at this audition, I can try again."

## Extreme versus Normal Stress Reactions

So, will your brain always turn down your stress response when you pay attention to messages from your alarm? Training your thinking center to pay attention to your alarm's signals always begins the process of resetting your amygdala. But reducing stress is a learning process for all of us. If you have an extreme stress reaction, or if you've been suffering from extreme stress for years, even your whole life, you need to give yourself room and be prepared to be patient as you begin to intentionally activate your learning brain.

That's why we want to differentiate between the two kinds of stress reactions. You can't instantly return a brain to optimal function after extreme stress. An *extreme stress reaction* is when the alarm takes control and overwhelms the learning brain. It can happen after traumatic events that result in PTSD, or it can be the result of long-term chronic stress. In either case, in a chronic stress reaction, the brain's alarm is triggered too fast, too often, and too strongly for the person to be able to cope effectively and think clearly.

One of the most common cases of extreme stress occurs in men and women returning from combat. It has been commonly observed, by scientists and by family members and friends, that individuals returning from battles zones who saw the worst of war tended to find the minor stresses of home life harder to deal with than the life-and-death trauma of fighting. Just going to the grocery store may cause a veteran more stress reactions than being under enemy fire.

This happens for two reasons. First, military personnel train themselves not to pay attention to signals from their brain's alarm when in combat, except for the really urgent ones that involve immediate life-threatening danger. Second, the ordinary stressors in civilian life often are due to problems that, while much less dangerous, actually are harder to solve than those in war. Soldiers need to react rapidly and competently when people behave erratically in combat. It can be harder to know how to respond when a rude person cuts you off in line, though both situations trigger a similar alarm reaction.

Another common problem for military veterans is driving. Imagine heavy traffic in a city like Boston, Massachusetts. Boston is divided from Cambridge by the Charles River. Running along the river is a road, Storrow Drive. It is one of the major thoroughfares for commuters, delivery drivers, and tourists traveling between the restaurants, businesses, and historic sites in Boston, and Harvard University and MIT in Cambridge. Some of the most common vehicles on this road are white vans; some of the vehicles most commonly used by suicide bombers in Iraq and Afghanistan are white vans.

Suddenly a white van cuts off the veteran and his wife. The veteran screams, "Watch out!" He starts to sweat. He grabs the door handle, pinned down to his seat. In that moment, his brain thinks he's about to be blown up as he saw happen to friends overseas. There's nothing he can do. The truck may be carrying flowers or cakes, but he can't pull the van over and investigate like he could at war. The driver may have been talking on his cell phone or simply wasn't paying attention, but the veteran perceives it as a personal threat, and his hyperactive alarm means he may not be able to calm down for the rest of the night.

We all can appreciate how easily traffic sets off our alarms. But for most of us, it's a *normal stress reaction*. A normal stress reaction occurs when the alarm and the thinking and memory centers work together. The adrenaline rush dissipates naturally because the learning brain recognizes the true nature of the threat—the traffic isn't putting us in danger. The learning brain can access similar events from the memory center when you were cut off and got to your destination safely, as well as the personal resources you've used before to handle situations when you've been surprised in traffic.

Being cut off still might startle a person with a normal stress reaction. That's appropriate because it causes you to slow down, check the surrounding traffic for problems, and make sure you're safe. The stress reaction lets you notice your alarm, pay attention, and then quickly go back to a normal state. All that *usually* happens without you even thinking about it. You just notice your stress rising and then falling. Even in normal stress reactions, it's important to realize that an adrenaline rush *does* cascade through the body. It may take a few minutes to feel comfortable again, even when you know everything is all right. There is, however, a key difference between an extreme and normal stress reaction: in a normal stress reaction the brain is learning, rather than just surviving.

## The Signs of a Learning Brain

We know our learning brains are in control, keeping the alarm's activity at a level appropriate to what we're doing in a given moment when we can

- stop and think before taking action
- think clearly when relaxed or when under pressure
- enjoy a challenge and end up better for having taken it on
- savor quiet moments without needing to seek stimulation
- reflect about what we want to take away from an experience
- take pleasure in a quiet conversation with a friend or family member
- solve a problem creatively
- respond rapidly to an immediate need without distress
- practice a skill while paying attention to every step until it's second nature
- absorb the "take home message" from a class or book
- listen to what others say with interest and respect for their point of view
- change a worry into a plan that makes things better for everyone
- recognize the difference between a fact and an assumption

This probably describes you some, even most of the time. All of us have used our learning brains many times in our lives. But sometimes, when trying to do things that are most important to us, our alarms still get in the way.

*So* what's different in our brains when we're learning? Where do calm and confidence come from?

Most of us think that people who are calm and confident are just good at being relaxed or have high self-esteem. Both can happen naturally. Some people's bodies instinctively reset the alarm most of the time. But more than likely, at the moment of calmness, a person who appears to have it all together has learned to think clearly even in times of heightened stress. Even for people who appear confident, it takes work and intention to apply their brain's innate capacity to focus on what they want to achieve.

And the person who seems naturally calm and confident isn't always in control. Every human being has times when we react, when we get angry, impulsive, or afraid. We just may not be around when the person we admire for their ability to be in control melts down. There are many ways to focus your thinking, but the common denominator is shifting your thoughts from what's wrong or what you "have to do," to what is truly most important. In every case, calm, confident people have learned to let the thinking center do its job.

## Thinking Clearly as a Community

Just as we can use our learning brains to turn down our alarms as individuals, communities have the power to help children learn from their earliest years how to reduce stress and discover personal control, even in the most caustic environments. We've cared for children and teenagers in the juvenile justice system, in children's programs in urban environments like the Humboldt Park Neighborhood of Chicago and the South Bronx neighborhood of New York, and we've helped children through the worst traumas like abuse and witnessing violence.

One of the greatest risks to the future of our world is insecurity. The constant triggers activating our children's alarms—images of violence in the media, economic insecurity, pressure at school from the earliest age, and neighborhoods that just aren't safe—threaten the development of their learning brains at a time when they need to discover how to think clearly and focus.

Vulnerable kids in both developing countries and countries with advanced economies need safe spaces and relationships to reach any kind of potential as thinkers and human beings. Children that are always stressed will struggle to learn clear thinking. Which is why the Harlem Children's Zone (HCZ) is one of the successful stories, a role model, in the fight against urban poverty. HCZ has helped to create an environment where young people develop a learning brain that is capable of overcoming even the most horrendous stress.

In the 1980s and 1990s, the problem in the Harlem borough of New York had a one-word name: crack. It's a chicken and egg debate as to whether drugs create poverty or poverty creates a culture of drug use, but what's undeniable is that the open-air drug markets, disintegrating housing, underemployment, and the violence that accompanies desperate people whose alarms are always turned up meant that kids couldn't learn. The schools were already underperforming, and the added cultural disintegration threatened an entire generation of children.

Then in the early 1990s, an experiment began in one block. The strategy was to provide health care, violence prevention, social services, small classrooms, and extended days to students from the beginning of a child's education. Then it expanded to twenty-four blocks.

The learning opportunities began for kids before they were even born. The HCZ offered a baby college course for expecting parents so that moms were ready to help their kids learn in their first months. Kindergarten lasted all day so children with working parents wouldn't be alone and vulnerable at home. Peacemakers, who were trained teaching assistants ready to help solve conflicts, worked in the schools to keep kids focused. College counseling, SAT prep, and career counseling pushed teens toward higher education.

The HCZ is now a ninety-seven-block area of the Harlem neighborhood, including 17,000 kids, with a clear goal: that every single child goes to college. Ninety percent of the participants in HCZ after-school programs went to college in 2011. When kids learn to manage their alarms from an early age and they have an environment that keeps their brains focused on learning, they know how to focus their thinking. With support and goals like college, the stress that gets in the way of development doesn't prevent them from accomplishing what matters most to them and their families.

Every organization, community, or country is successful only to the extent that it is able to create an environment that encourages and enables its members to act based on a core set of values rather than just survive. A primary reason why children fail to learn, businesses underperform, and entire countries spend years, even decades, in political and armed conflict is that they don't know how to balance survival imperatives that are driven by the alarm with the focused attention that activates their learning brains.

What the HCZ has done is switch the focus of an entire community from survival to learning. That doesn't mean there aren't debates about the organization's methods or how it will maintain its mission. That doesn't mean it won't have critics in and out of the community. It means the conversation has changed. Instead of alarm-based debates about safety and survival, now the conversation is focused on how to make every child's life worth living and fulfilled.

## Getting Out of Survival Mode

We can be intelligent, capable, and outwardly successful, we can have the greatest relationships in the world, and yet we can still be trapped in survival mode most of the time. We just don't realize it. We think we're relaxed, but really our brains are still on high alert, scanning for danger. In this state our brains instruct our bodies to pump out the stress chemicals that make us feel pressured, frustrated, or depressed, all in an attempt to make us more alert and aware.

How is this possible? How can talented professionals, capable parents, and the people we look up to actually be stressed all the time? The answer is not a personal weakness or shortcoming. It's a universal human dilemma. We all have an alarm in our brains, and if we don't know how to recognize and deal with the alarm, it will keep us perpetually stressed.

The solution is not rocket science, or even brain science. If our alarms are simply trying to get us to pay attention, the answer to the riddle of persistent stress is simply *to pay attention to the alarm and learn from what it's telling us.*

But here's the catch. Most of us think that we are paying attention to what matters when we let our minds get caught up in the problems or distress that drive our alarms to trigger stress reactions. What we're talking about is different. Paying attention by focusing our brain on learning is what satisfies the alarm and allows it to *turn itself down*.

Persistent, intolerable stress is not primarily due to an overactive alarm in the brain. An overactive alarm is the result of an underperforming learning brain. Few of us have been taught to optimize our brains.

# Chapter Three

# The Goal: Cultivate an Optimal Brain

Every human brain has the ability to focus, to zero in on what's most important at this moment. Even those of us who struggle with attention deficits or learning disabilities can find ways to pay attention to what we really care about. Except when a person has had a serious brain injury or has a disease such as Alzheimer's that damages the brain, stress reactions don't happen because our brains are faulty or broken (and even in those tragic cases, there are ways to achieve a focused state of mind). Stress reactions happen because we *aren't making the fullest use* of our brains' incredible power to optimize the relationship between the survival and learning brain.

Learning to focus begins by paying attention to stress. Just thinking about stress—not trying to fix it or make it go away—activates your learning brain. Ignoring stress only makes it worse, and you miss an opportunity to activate your thinking center and help your alarm to quiet down.

So let's practice again.

Measure your stress level on a scale of one to ten, ten being that a catastrophic event just happened to you and one being a state of total calm. We hope it is low because you've stepped back from your life and immersed yourself in learning about your brain.

Now measure your level of personal control on a scale of one to ten, ten being totally clear thinking and one being complete confusion. We hope it is high, maybe a six, seven, or even higher as you consider how you can use what you're reading to make your life better.

If your stress level is low and your level of personal control is high, the reason is simple: you've chosen to focus on learning how your brain really works. Like Dorothy when she peeked behind the curtain and saw the Wizard of Oz, you're figuring out the relationship between the alarm, memory center, and thinking center. This engagement of the learning brain optimizes the connection with the alarm.

If you are feeling some stress as you learn, however, that would be normal too. Learning is engaging, even exciting. When your learning brain focuses on something that is important to you, your level of arousal goes up. You care about what you're doing, so your alarm simultaneously keeps you energized. It doesn't want your mind to wander. It wants you to pay attention so you can absorb the material.

It almost seems paradoxical: stress can be a good thing. It is. The alarm wants the learning brain to be ready to step in and take control, so it can relax and reset itself. You need the survival brain to produce the stress reactions that signal your learning brain to wake up and maintain or regain your focus.

It is the focus on learning that optimizes our brain and frees us from stress. Learning happens when the thinking center communicates to the alarm, "I'm figuring out what's really important here, and I've got it handled." This message enables the alarm to know that indeed everything is under control.

Our brains are not broken when we have extreme stress reactions; it's operator error. We're reacting to the charge of the alarm when we need to translate its message into a renewed search for what's important.

## The Optimal Brain

Optimizing the relationship between the alarm of the survival brain and the thinking and memory centers of the learning brain is the key not only to reducing stress, but more importantly to being able to use our brain to accomplish what we really want in life. Optimizing how our brains function begins with understanding how the brain is organized.

As Abraham Maslow discovered, we have a hierarchy of needs—we need to have certain basic necessities like food and shelter before we can pursue other, higher essentials, like love and social harmony. Similarly, there is a hierarchy in our brains.

The brain has three basic levels. The first is the bridge that connects the body to the survival brain. At the bottom of the brain—literally, beginning at the top of the spinal cord at the base of your skull, and extending up into the lower mid-section of the brain—is what researchers describe as the *reptile brain*. Reptiles' brains actually include only these areas and neither of the two higher levels found in humans.

The reptile brain is the body's life-support system, ensuring it receives enough oxygen, food, and liquids to stay alive. It sends chemical (via hormones) and electrical messages (via the nervous system) to activate and coordinate the body when we do anything physical, including walking, talking, sleeping, eating, and having sex. The reptile brain is designed to work automatically like a robot, without any thought or choice. It is not designed to protect us from danger, only to keep our basic bodily functions intact.

The second level is deep in the middle of the brain, and just above the reptile brain. Scientists have described this middle area as the *paleo-mammalian* brain because all mammals, from the humblest tree shrew to the most advanced species (human beings), have this additional capacity. The paleomammalian brain has been called the *emotional brain* because it includes the alarm, the reward centers, and several other nearby areas that enable us to feel basic emotions such as fear and anger as well as happiness and satisfaction.

The emotional brain has two responsibilities. First, it contains the brain's alarm center, which keeps us alert and protects us from danger. The alarm in this mid-section teams up with the reptilian brain below it to keep us alive—together, they are the survival brain.

The second role of the middle part of the brain is to get us to pay attention to the next priority after survival—pleasure. The brain's reward centers can make life enjoyable by focusing our attention on things, activities, and people that give us enjoyment. But they also can make life miserable by pressuring us to go after rewards even when there are high costs for doing so, like addiction and dangerous risks.

The reward centers are relevant to stress because they lie next to the alarm centers and the two often communicate. When they function well together, they make life richer and more fulfilling. When they work at cross-purposes, however, the emotional brain can cause us a great deal of stress. When the alarm and reward centers push us in different directions, the result can be a state of extreme stress. For instance, the reward center may demand that we go skydiving, while at the same time, the alarm will scream that it's not safe to jump out of a plane at 10,000 feet.

Thankfully, as humans we have a third level of the brain that allows us to think as well as react. The third and highest level, which is what we have been calling the learning brain, is the *neomammalian* brain. Only the most advanced mammals have a neomammalian brain: these primates include human beings and other mammals that can stand on two legs and use their arms and hands independently, such as apes and monkeys. Instead of merely obeying the commands of the emotional brain or relying on the reflexes and habits of the reptilian brain, the neomammalian brain enables us to make choices based upon thinking.

Located at the very top of the brain just below the skull, the neomammalian brain runs from the back all the way to the front of our head. Not surprisingly, it is the area where what we describe as the thinking center is found. The thinking center lies at the very front of the neomammalian brain in an area that is called the prefrontal cortex because it is at the top of our head (the cortex) and just behind (pre) the forehead (frontal).

The location is interesting and possibly not coincidental. As the topmost and furthest front area of the brain, the thinking center is the last area to get messages from the deeper reptile and emotional levels.

This has some benefits and costs. The thinking center gets the most information. It is the command center and the decision maker. But it gets the information last, after all other areas of the brain have a chance to add their input and react to the data. The thinking center also has to anticipate the future as it plans and makes choices, which requires a tremendous amount of energy.

In order to handle its responsibilities, the thinking center relies on the other parts of the brain for good information. The alarm and reward centers, however, are terrible at weeding out what is useful from that which is irrelevant. They tend to treat everything, no matter how minor, as a top priority. The reptile brain doesn't even know the thinking center exists.

As a result, the thinking center uses the brain's memory center to manage the demanding and urgent messages from the other levels. Even though the memory center is located far from the thinking center, its location is a plus because it can catch and filter the messages from the alarm and reward centers before they bombard the thinking center with too much information. The memory center screens messages, looking for those that are useful as the thinking center fulfills its executive functions. The learning brain, therefore, is a team effort led by the thinking center with the invaluable support and assistance of the memory center.

The optimum brain is a larger team; in addition to the learning brain, it includes the alarm and reward centers in the emotional brain and all our animal needs in the reptile brain. The main problem that can arise for this team is that the alarm and reward centers can become so demanding that they can distract or even overwhelm the memory center with a flood of intense messages.

This hierarchy is important because our alarms are always right in the middle of everything that happens in the brain. The alarm, which almost never sleeps, is almost always actively communicating with the reptilian brain; for example, it gives orders to speed up or slow down our heart rate and breathing, or to tense up or relax our muscles. And simultaneously it receives messages from the reptile brain about the safety, strength, and health of our body. Like a mousetrap set to go off, it will fire if it perceives we are in danger. The alarm also constantly sends messages to the memory center to pull up files that can help us to pay attention, either to dangers or to potential rewards.

To optimize our brains we need to be able to recognize, rather than ignore, messages from all levels. For this to happen, the alarm has to know for sure that we are thinking clearly enough to be safe. The reward centers can't provide this message, because they'll run us off a cliff if that will bring us pleasure. The memory center can't reassure the alarm, because it provides information from our memory files without making judgements or decisions.

It is only the thinking center which can both process the information from the reptile and emotional brain, and then switch our focus to what we want to learn. We can choose the level of stress in our body so that it keeps us focused on what we want to achieve. *As thinking is our brains' greatest power, our ability to use it is our greatest opportunity to reduce stress.* To illustrate how a brain can optimize itself, let's look at an example of a young woman who used her brain to achieve peak performance, in the realm of physical strength, artistic excellence, and mental focusing.

## The Secret Ingredient in Peak Performance

The major barrier to peak performance is not a lack of physical, creative, or mental ability. It is a brain in which survival and learning have become enemies rather than competitive partners. People who achieve peak performance optimize not only their bodies and their technical skills and knowledge, but also their minds. They are intuitively able to focus their thinking centers on both learning from their alarms and communicating to their alarms that their thinking centers are in control. Or, they developed this ability through mentors and role models who showed them how to focus.

In the 2002 Winter Olympics in Salt Lake City, Utah, the skating world was ready to finally crown another princess. At twenty-two, Michelle Kwan had won four World Championships and six U.S. Championships. She had already earned a silver medal in the 1998 Olympics in Nagano, Japan, where she narrowly lost the gold to fellow American Tara Lipinski.

After the short program, the first of two skates from which the judges award the gold, Kwan was in the lead. In fourth place was Sarah Hughes, the bronze medal winner from the U.S. Championships. Hughes was not a newcomer to the international scene, but Kwan was still the favorite. Her entire life had been focused on winning this one competition, which had eluded her.

What happened before the first skate of the competition is a fascinating study in optimizing the brain. Before the short program, Kwan was smiling. She had learned from her past experiences how to focus on the present. In her comments after the first night she said, "I'm proud to be an American and I tried to skate from my heart, tried to make Americans proud. It was an incredible moment for me." She was certainly nervous, but she used her learning brain to focus on what she could control and that turned down her alarm.

Hughes, on the other hand, was having a full-on alarm reaction that first night. As she waited to begin, she looked down and skated in circles. When she tried to take a deep breath, her shoulders rose noticeably with the tightness. It wasn't until she finished her jumps, which were imperfect, but solid, that she started to smile.

Notice the difference in their alarms. Kwan knew how to handle the nerves and anticipation. She understood that, for her, focusing on the pleasure of representing her country and skating from her heart was the way to let her alarm know that her learning brain was in control. Hughes was sixteen and comparatively inexperienced. It was her first Olympics, and she lost to the two other Americans at the U.S. Championships. She couldn't turn down her alarm, and simply fought her way through the adrenaline.

And then, something changed.

A few nights later, Hughes described how she went out for the long skate. "I didn't want to skate for a gold medal. I went out and had a great time. I said, 'This is the Olympics. I want to do the best.'" In between performances she had optimized her brain.

She smiled before beginning her routine. She hit her first double and smoothly flowed across the ice. Then, she hit her first triple, in fact, a combination of two triple jumps, and the moment she landed you could see her alarm reset. She couldn't help a wide smile. And in each jump after, the same thing: intense focus on her face before the jump and then total jubilation when she landed it. When she finished, she beamed with pleasure. "I skated for pure enjoyment," she said. "That's how I wanted my Olympic moment to be."

Kwan, who had managed her alarm so well the night before, skated second to last for the long program. Maybe it was Hughes performing before her. Maybe it was the pressure of four years waiting for another chance at gold. She looked focused before the skate, and smiled wide before the music started. But her first jump was tight. The next triple was a failed, two-footed landing. Then, at three minutes into her program, she fell.

"I think I was a little more disappointed in Nagano, just because I skated much better," Kwan said later. "Tonight it was one of those things. I don't know what didn't go my way."

Their focus was the difference.

For Kwan, the alarm goal of winning took over in the final performance. The desire to feel the pleasure of her lifelong dream overwhelmed her learning brain's ability to focus on what was really most important: enjoying a skate at the Olympics.

The second night Hughes, who was tight her first skate, became more and more free with each successful jump. As she focused on the pleasure of being an Olympian, each successive landing gave her a greater sense of control. Her brain, pulling up memories of all the tens of thousands of jumps she'd landed in practice, raised her ability to think clearly about getting ready for each new leap. With Kwan, her alarm roared louder and louder with each mistake and she did not have the ability to turn it down.

In both cases, the secret to their great performances was using their learning brains to listen to and then show the alarm that they were in control. Each was able to be completely focused: Hughes simply did it better at the most critical moment.

## A Shift in Focus

True focus is paying attention to what's important and not letting a heightened alarm reaction become a substitute for thinking. When you ask yourself, "What's really most important to me in life?" do you find that the first answers that come to mind are problems? Do you worry you'll never get what you want most? Or do you think of situations or people who make you crazy?

These are normal thoughts, but they won't help you achieve peak performance or a life you actually want to live. They are reactions based upon messages from your brain's alarm, telling you what's blocking you from achieving what's most important to you. In addition to figuring out solutions to problems, or avoiding them and hoping things will somehow miraculously get better, what can you do?

Signaling your brain's alarm that it doesn't need to worry *because you recognize its concerns and are able to handle the situation* requires a shift in focus. The shift moves you from being driven by the problem messages to choosing to focus on what you want you learn.

In an optimum brain, the first things you think of when your alarm signals you are core

- emotions (such as love, trust, and confidence)
- thoughts (such as your fundamental values)
- goals (such as what we aim to achieve in order to live up to those values)
- choices (being empathetic or respectful rather than argumentative or defensive)

In an optimum brain, you take what you've learned in your life that is most important to you and use that to guide you, rather than letting your alarm make all the choices based only on survival (or fleeting rewards).

And you do it all day every day, not just occasionally. You dedicate yourself daily to remembering what gives your life value, in large ways (such as taking time to pray or purposefully doing things that aren't easy but that make the world a better place) and small ways (such as stopping to think before you let irritation spill over onto other people).

Is an optimum brain possible for all of us? Or do you have to be an Olympian with a team of coaches to learn how to focus? Yes, it is possible, and it doesn't require a team of coaches. Every human brain is gifted with the possibility for optimum performance.

No one is born with the ability to bring the survival and learning brains together as a team. Focus is learned and developed. It takes determination, dedication, and repeated practice. But it's no harder to learn than any other skill.

## Homefront Heroes

Parents and families use the same set of skills that produce peak performance every day. One of the most striking examples is the spouses and partners of military men and women. As their loved ones risk their lives overseas, these homefront heroes focus on their children's health and education, the family's finances, and providing a stable home environment. Many also take on the added responsibility of working outside the home.

How? How do they not constantly melt down when their partners are in a war zone and they have to manage a household, their own worries and fears, and support the person they love when he or she is so far away? They activate their learning brains by focusing on what's most important.

When Mary Beth's husband was set to deploy for Afghanistan October 1, she knew exactly what to do. The family's favorite holiday was Thanksgiving. It was the one time when both her and her husband's parents came to their house to celebrate with their three young children. So she threw the traditional feast in September. By gathering her whole family early, she not only gave them a memory to hold onto while he was away, she made the time they had together as rich as it could be.

No one is able to activate their learning brain perfectly, or all the time. These men and women feel angry and depressed. They say things without thinking—just like any one of us would if we dealt with the load of stressors they face under even the best of circumstances. But while their partners are in harm's way they can make an invaluable contribution by being the person who makes the family and home—including their own health and well-being—as secure as it can be.

They are often the unsung heroes of war, because with courage and dedication they switch their focus from stress to love. Optimizing their brain doesn't take away the ache of separation or the anxiety of not knowing whether their partners are safe. But by tapping into their learning brain, they make meaning out of the pain. They switch their focus to what's precious, and give their soldiers the support and reassurance that makes the difference between being constantly in alarm mode and being highly focused.

## Borrowing a Learning Brain: Mount Everest, Part I

As military personnel need their spouses and partners to help them turn down their alarms during deployments, sometimes we all rely on others to provide the learning brains we need when we feel trapped by ongoing stress.

Think of your favorite coach or teacher. The best coaches are like John Wooden, who loaned his learning brain to his players with short, corrective bursts of advice. The most impactful teachers are like the poet Maya Angelou, who gives dozens of lectures a year, reminding audiences about the diversity of life and culture, something every person can focus on. When someone else helps us focus on what we can do in the moment, they calm our alarms by teaching our learning brains to send the clear message: we have something more important to do right now than be stressed.

The people we'd least expect can achieve amazing things when they have others to help them learn to focus. Before 2010, the youngest person to ever reach the top of Mount Everest had been a sixteen-year-old Nepalese climber. When Jordan Romero was thirteen, in May of 2010, he set the world record for the youngest climber ever to reach the summit. With his father and stepmom, both experienced mountaineers, he reached a peak at 29,029 feet.

How is that possible? Most teenagers can't keep their brain focused enough to do their algebra homework. What made it possible for Jordan to endure the discomfort that has killed over two hundred people out of the more than five thousand ascents on the peak?

Undoubtedly his training and preparation was rigorous and extensive. We don't know exactly what went through his mind at every stage in the ascent, but what we do know is that he had a dream. His goal was to climb the highest peaks on every continent. But that wouldn't have been enough. He didn't only want to conquer the mountains. He wanted to do something so amazing that it would be a source of pride and confidence for the rest of his life. He was showing that a person, no matter the age, could take on what seemed to be an impossible challenge.

But even that wouldn't have been enough for a teenager to achieve such an enormous goal. Most importantly for his brain, he didn't climb alone. He had a deep sense of trust and confidence in his father and stepmother. The family is from Big Bear Lake, California, and climbing is their lifestyle. In addition to their technical mountaineering skills, Jordan trusted his parents to push him without pushing him into something he didn't want to do. He said, in an interview on *The Today Show*, that there were times when he wanted to quit; and the family kept climbing because they wanted, as a family, to do what no other family had done.

We can always borrow a learning brain from a friend, family, teachers, coaches, and therapists when our alarms blare. Whether we want to learn to do something new that scares us, or remove the pain of stress in a busy life, we don't have to reclaim our brains and their ability to focus alone.

All of us can lose sight of our core values and goals in the midst of an alarm reaction. Each of us, however, has the capacity, even the responsibility, to regain our focus on those values and goals at some point. When we respectfully acknowledge the gift provided by the other person who stayed in learning mode and helped us refocus, we realize the power of the optimal brain. Even more exciting, we prepare ourselves to lend our learning brains to someone else in the future.

## Integrating Survival and Learning to Optimize the Brain

The approach to optimizing the brain that we'll show you in the rest of this book is based on a set of skills that Julian teaches in his clinical and research work with adults, adolescents, and children who have been traumatized or have been dealing with chronic life stress. A client asked him at one point to take those skills and find a single word that could be used to remember them easily.

As he thought about that creative request, Julian realized that the dilemma that every person faces when traumatized or stressed is being trapped in an alarm state. As terrible as some traumas and stressors can be, the worst part of the experience usually is the years or decades afterward, when the stress reactions never seem to get better.

Even though extreme stress reactions can begin as a necessary way to survive a traumatic experience, when they persist and even minor stressors trigger these "post-traumatic stress" reactions, they can become a terrible trap. PTSD is a condition that occurs because the brain becomes stuck in survival mode long after the trauma has ended. Survivors don't know how to stop their brains from trying to protect them. Julian decided that the word that best described the path to a better life was FREEDOM.

We all wish that we could be free of trauma and stress. While there are many inspiring initiatives worldwide dedicated to preventing violence, abuse, discrimination, extreme poverty, and the breakdown of society, trauma and stress will never be eradicated completely. What we can do is change the way we respond to trauma and stress and the way we restore our lives after traumatic and stressful experiences.

The letters in the acronym FREEDOM stand for a model of optimizing your brain that we're about to teach you. The letters stand for

- **F**ocusing
- **R**ecognizing triggers
- **E**mpowering your emotions
- **E**xercising your core values
- **D**etermining your optimal goals
- **O**ptimizing your choices
- **M**aking a positive contribution to the world

We've introduced you to the key role that focusing plays in dealing with stress and optimizing the brain, and in the next part we'll introduce you to a practical way to cultivate and practice that skill. You'll be amazed at how often you are already capable of this way of thinking, which makes this skill easy to learn. And you'll also be amazed by how many opportunities you have each day to focus and make choices that turn down the alarm in your brain and other people's brains. This is one of the most valuable contributions that any person can make.

Then each subsequent chapter will reveal how to focus under extreme stress, what to focus on to optimize your brain, and the personal control you have each day to choose the path of your life. We want you to learn the ways to focus your learning brain because your alarm will not stop sounding. We want you to feel free because you know listening to your alarm will start to turn it down. Your alarm knows when your life is out of balance, and we're about to show you how to use its signals to manage stress by focusing on what matters most in your life.

# Secondhand Stress: A Warning before We Move On

*Why is optimizing your brain so important?*

Secondhand stress. Even if you completely understand the science of your brain, even if you know the first thing to do any time you feel stressed, even if you practice the skills we're about to teach you to the point where you could teach a class or write a book yourself, it will not change the reality of the world we live in. In every environment you enter, someone else's alarm is going off, or it will.

Another person's alarm is like secondhand smoke. When someone next to you smokes, it affects the air you breathe too. If a building is on fire and you rush in without an oxygen mask, you will inhale the noxious gas. The same is true with stress.

You can be sitting at home, completely comfortable reading a book in your favorite chair, and unless you turn off every machine—television, radio, cell, smart phone, landline, and computer—other people can reach you. A friend can text you a simple message like, "Help!" They might just need help with a new recipe they're trying, but it can trigger your alarm, making you think they are in mortal peril.

Even shopping can create secondhand stress. A trip to the market is the kind of thing Europeans do daily. It is the kind of ritual they use to turn down their alarms. They walk between stalls carefully choosing the perfect produce, breads, and proteins for the day.

Now consider the modern American shopping experience that is slowly creeping across the planet. Everything, everything, everything is available for you now, Now, NOW!

The lights are bright. People rush. The goal is not to consider the precious commodity food is, but to sell you as much as possible in the least number of minutes so the greatest number of shoppers can get through a store each day. Did we just turn your alarm on with that last sentence?

That's the way secondhand stress works. Even if you have truly figured out how to free yourself from stress, that doesn't mean other people will do the same thing. Before we teach you what you need to know to truly manage your brain, we want you to understand that it will not suddenly free you from your friends who are drama queens or your office environment that is hectic and nerve-racking.

We never want you to forget that you can be aware of how much of an impact secondhand stress has on every person's life. Everyone has an alarm, and most people have no idea about how it works and how to reset it. Therefore, most of the people that we're around most of the time are having or on the verge of having alarm reactions. They're not bad people, they just don't realize how their alarms drive their lives.

We'll teach you what to do in circumstances when your alarm gets fired up by other people's alarm reactions, when your reactions to secondhand stress threaten to overwhelm your thinking and memory centers. Then you'll know that the solution is not to blame people for making their stress reactions your stress reactions—because we all do that at times. Instead, what we want you to realize is that you can intentionally use your optimal brain to help them and you. Not by giving them a lecture about how their brain's alarm is making your life miserable—that would be your alarm taking over. Instead, you can reset your alarm, and show the other person that it is possible to shift from survival mode to feeling calm and thinking clearly.

There are many stresses that we can and must learn to live with. And there are other stresses in our lives that we need to remove or be removed from. In both cases, handling the stress requires an optimal brain. That happens when you know how to keep the pathway open between your alarm and your thinking center. Fortunately, all of us do this each day when we focus, and we can learn to do it intentionally.

# Part II

The Missing First Step in
Stress Management:
Focusing

# Chapter Four

# A Brief Introduction to SOS

Having introduced you to what the optimum brain is capable of, and the reality that in every moment you can reset your alarm by focusing on what really matters to you, now we're going to show you how. The first step of the FREEDOM model is Focusing.

We know we're supposed to focus—on our families, on our work, and on things like sports or music that we want to master. But how do we focus our minds?

The most efficient formula for focusing can be described with a familiar term: SOS. SOS is generally known as the universal call for help, the shorthand that maritime captains send by Morse code when a ship is sinking. In the FREEDOM model, SOS has a similar but different meaning. Each letter reminds you to do something that is essential for your brain to focus. SOS stands for Step back, Orient, and Self-check. It is a simple technique that you can use any time you experience unwanted or potentially unmanageable stress reactions, or when you simply want to be at your best. It is the way you can turn down your alarm and think clearly again.

The problem with most stress management tools is that even though they precisely describe what to do, they will not work unless they enable you to create a partnership between the alarm and your learning brain. That partnership can happen by accident when you use a stress management technique, but to be consistent you need to know how to make it happen.

SOS is a scientifically validated practice that reduces stress in two ways. First, it is a *preventive measure*. To prevent stress reactivity, in which your brain's alarm gets out of hand like the Hulk's, you need to train your mind to prepare for stressful situations and see stress coming before it triggers more than a mild and easily manageable stress reaction.

SOS is also an *intervention* to interrupt and calm alarm reactions when they occur. Your alarm is designed to alert and protect you by reacting. Your alarm knows that trouble can occur in your life, and it wants to make sure that nothing bad happens to you in the future—or at least that you're ready for future stressors if they can't be prevented. When you master SOS though, you'll rarely need to use it as an intervention because you'll recognize an alarm reaction in its early stages and know where and how to focus before stress hijacks your brain.

## Step Back, Orient, and Self-Check: A New SOS

The first "S" is for *step back*. To step back is to be present. It is to pause, slow down, and clear the mind of the swirling thoughts that often escalate in times of stress. The first move in opening the pathway between the alarm and the learning brain is to return the mind to a place of calm, comfortable alertness. Remember, to think clearly and be mentally focused, it is essential not only to be relaxed and ready to learn, but also to heed the call of the brain's alarm to be alert. Stepping back is a way to accomplish both goals simultaneously. It optimizes the brain's activity almost instantly. See if you can experience it right now.

Pause for ten seconds and sweep your mind clear of every thought.

Could you do it? Most of us can't at first. Many of us struggle to do something as ordinary as making coffee without a thousand thoughts swirling through our minds. When we can slow down, totally present in what we're experiencing, we've begun to switch our focus from the brain's alarm to its thinking center.

Let's try to step back again.

Your mind has the ability to take you to your earliest memories or another imagined part of the universe in the blink of an eye. Yet in this instant, you are in a specific location. When the mind just won't empty or thoughts and images flood back despite your intention to sweep them away, another way to step back is to pay attention to the environment surrounding you or your own body. You can always look, listen, and feel the place you're in.

To begin the process, look around you and just observe whatever you notice. Don't judge, evaluate, or try to make changes, just observe. Wherever you are, for ten seconds, pause and look.

Now do it again, but this time, close your eyes and just listen.

In both cases, you began to open up the pathways between the different levels of your brain. When you stepped back, you slowed your mind and became present.

Now you're ready for the "O" in SOS: *orient*. To orient is to make a single, clear—but not easy—choice. The choice can be found in answering this question: what is the one thought that expresses what is most important to you in your life right now? That's it. A thought is any kind of mental activity. Different examples of thinking include images, visualizations, an idea, a word or phrase, an emotion, a value, or a goal. The key to reducing stress is literally to focus on *one thing* in the present that is most important to you in your life at this very moment.

This usually takes some preparation because it is essential to hone in on an aspect of your life that has the greatest value in a positive sense, not the problem or challenge that you're most obsessed with. A common error in SOS is to focus on a thought that really is an alarm issue rather than an optimal thought that turns down the alarm. For instance, when you focus on what you don't want to do, like not wanting to make a mistake in a game or not wanting to say the wrong thing in a presentation, you actually raise your alarm.

You'll know if you've done that because you won't be able to hold that thought without having more negative thoughts or a physical stress reaction. The thoughts we'll teach you to find are the ones that give you a sense of calm and the control that comes from thinking clearly. So what's that thought right now?

Is it to learn something that you're deeply interested in?

Is it to be with someone you value? Or imagine being with them or hearing their voice?

Is it to do something that you find deeply rewarding?

Is it to know something about yourself that gives you a genuine sense of pride?

Step back again for ten seconds.

Now focus on this one thought: I am a person of value because I _____.

Read that last phrase a few more times.

You just did the first two steps of SOS. You switched your focus to the present by using your thinking center to decide what you wanted to pay attention to. When you sweep your mind clear, or just observe where you are and what your body is feeling, you exercise your ability to be mentally in control. This provides your alarm with feedback showing that you are alert and aware, which enables it to begin turning down the feeling of being stressed.

Then you can directly activate your thinking center. You can use it to create a new idea that is most important to you, like focusing on this book's message, or use it to send a message to your memory center to retrieve a feeling or idea from your past. It can only be one thought or the alarm will sound again. But when you identify one thought—whether this is a word or sentence, an image or sound, or an activity, place, or person—what *you choose* to think about or remember shows the alarm you're totally in control.

But sometimes, it doesn't work.

That's why the third step in SOS is a second "S": *self-check*. Each time you do SOS, the final step that closes the loop and ensures you learned from the activity is to do a simple numerical rating of your stress level on a scale from one to ten. As we talked about in the opening chapter, ten is a major alarm reaction, the most stressed or distressed you've ever felt in your life. At the other end of the scale, one is a place of total calm and freedom from any stress. The stress self-check is a way to take your alarm's temperature. The majority of the time, most of us have a stress level somewhere between three and eight—rarely totally stress free or at the peak of stress.

If you're in that middle range, between three and eight on the stress scale, the best way to focus your mind is to make a mental note (or write a note in a journal) of your stress level and then move on to checking your level of personal control. You want to keep track of the experiences that raise your alarm so you can handle them differently next time. However, if your stress level is very high, a nine or even a ten (the worst you've ever felt in your life), it's important to pause and decide what you can do to deal with serious threats or problems immediately.

After checking your level of stress, it's also important to self-check your level of personal control. A ten means that your mind is so focused that you feel in total control of your life. A one means that your mind is so unfocused that your thinking center is not working at all and you feel out of control or unable to think clearly. As with the stress self-check, the personal control ratings usually are somewhere between three and eight for most people, meaning that you have some personal control based on thinking clearly but not complete control. If that's the case, then make a mental note (or, again, a written one if you're a diary-keeper).

However, if your personal control level is very low, a two or even a one, it's best to step back and deal with the immediate situation. Usually, when personal control is at its lowest levels, it's not because you really have no control or are totally out of control (with the exception of extreme disasters or personal traumas that shut down the thinking center). It's because the alarm has filled your body with adrenaline that prevents you from thinking clearly.

What gets us back into our "right minds" is the same thing that enables us to recover from extreme stress reactions. We need to activate our thinking centers and shift our focus to learning. If you're at a one or two in personal control, step back again, and reorient your mind by focusing on just one core thought that helps you remember what your life really is all about. You may still feel upset or shaken, but now you'll find that you can start to figure things out rather than simply reacting.

When you can routinely step back, orient, and self-check your alarm and your ability to think clearly, you develop a skill that used to be reserved for the great mystics and Sufis. Only the most successful performers in business, the arts, and sports mastered it, and they learned it intuitively. The best part about SOS is that it becomes your new habit when you face stress. Not only do you feel less stress because you're ready for stressful moments, you know what to do as you feel your alarm rising.

It's impossible to do a twenty-minute meditation in the middle of a tense board meeting and your spouse might not appreciate you suddenly taking up a yoga position in the middle of a fight. But you can do SOS.

## A Good Night's Sleep

Dennis couldn't sleep. The presentation was, quite simply, the most important of his life. His new baby was sleeping. His wife was sleeping. Dennis wasn't sleeping because they needed a new apartment with more than one bedroom. If the board liked his plan for the new product, his boss promised him a bigger bonus. It would be the money they needed to get a bigger space.

His thoughts raced. "What if I fail? I've presented to big groups hundreds of times. I'm a salesman. I can do this. But what if I get sick? What if I forget the most important points? I know boards like to interrupt in the middle of presentations: what if I can't jump to the right slide quick enough?

"I told Marci I'd get us a bigger place. She's going to think I'm a failure if I don't pull this off. Maybe I am a failure if they don't like the product."

Dennis looked at the ceiling, and then he remembered SOS. "I know I won't do well tomorrow if I don't get some sleep."

He stepped back. His favorite method was to listen to his new baby breathe. He rolled over, looked at her bassinet for a moment, closed his eyes, and listened.

Then he rolled on his back and smiled. He could already feel his stress level coming down. He decided to focus on the thing that had always calmed him down as a child: shooting baskets. He imagined himself shooting baskets. He did this for a few minutes, and it worked, mostly.

The thoughts about the presentation kept intruding. He checked his stress and it still was too high, down to a four, but not low enough to sleep. He'd practiced his talk so many times the last thing he wanted to do was practice again. What he desperately wanted was to feel the firm handshake of success. He wanted those board members to look him in the eye and tell him what a great job he'd done. "That's it," he thought, getting a bit excited.

To slow down again, he closed his eyes and listened to his daughter.

Then he imagined shaking their hands, the look of pleasure in their eyes. He thought about how proud his wife would be when she heard how well he had done. He could feel his breathing slow. He imagined being in the room, having done exactly what he knew he was capable of doing. He shook another board member's hand, and felt himself drift away.

## Why Do People Take Cigarette Breaks?

Most people do versions of SOS without even knowing it. Some of them, however, aren't actually healthy for our brains.

Gabrielle smokes. When she takes a break at work, she smokes. When she's in a fight with her boyfriend, she smokes. When she's out with her friends relaxing, she loves to enjoy a few cigarettes. When we asked her why, like many of our clients she said, "Because it makes me feel better." We hear people say that smoking makes them feel energized again and like they can face whatever is coming next. All the answers actually point to the same reality: smoking is an SOS.

You can literally turn down and reset the alarm in your brain. But instead of doing this by focusing on one thought that matters, many people, when faced with stress or ongoing stressors, smoke. When you smoke you have to step back by pulling the cigarette out of the pack and then carefully lighting it. You immediately focus on one thing: the feeling of inhaling and exhaling the gray air. Most smokers tell you that they immediately feel their stress level going down during or after smoking, even though nicotine is a stimulant.

The real reason they feel better is not the cigarette. It's that they're using the cigarette to do everything that is involved in SOS. The person who smokes is fully present, focused on one thing—enjoying smoking (or more likely, whatever they feel free enough to enjoy thinking about when a cigarette finally gives them an excuse to take a break). There's no magic to cigarettes; they're just a vehicle people use to focus their minds on what they want to think about. That's why they feel less stress and more control after smoking.

If it weren't so dangerous, it would be the ideal teaching tool. Because it is so difficult to learn how to regulate our alarms, many of us have become addicted to chemical replacements instead of true solutions to stress. Addictions like drinking and eating cause even more havoc when we just want to feel relief. They're largely the result of alarm reactions we haven't learned to manage.

But there is another option.

## The Two Worlds

*SOS is like turning on a light in the dark.*

Nothing's changed except the way your mind focuses, but the new focus changes what you can see and what you know. Too many of us think that stress reactions are the normal condition of life, and that stress-free moments happen randomly or by accident. We savor the memory of those moments: a romantic evening, a perfect vacation, competing at our best, or mastering a project.

Even though we want more of these moments that feel so good, we accept that normal life is just going to be unmanageably stressful. Your life doesn't have to be stressful all the time. You don't have to change the world to change your own stress reactions and how you deal with them.

There are two worlds you can experience in each new moment. Option one: *alarm world*. It is dark, and a place of pain and stress. It is a place of confusion, harboring the feeling that you're not in control. It is a place where you let your brain react rather than allowing the alarm to dictate your experience. It is a feeling of panic, powerlessness, fear, and desperation. It is a hopeless place where every day is a grind and the future is something you just don't want to think about. It's made worse by the brief periods of happiness that sooner or later end in even greater periods of stress.

Option two is the *optimal world*. After learning how to focus your mind, most days can be more like your best days, which used to happen by luck or accident. Instead of thoughts and emotions that trigger your alarm, you think about what you want to have in your head and you feel the emotions of your learning brain, not your alarm. You choose goals and experiences that don't flood your body with adrenaline and stress; instead, you live in a way that makes a contribution without putting impossible challenges and miserable burdens into each day.

Life in the optimal world isn't perfect. But when your alarm works in harmony with your thinking and memory center, you have an optimal brain that enables you to choose how you face real challenges when they arise. When urgent needs lead your alarm to send out stress signals, you'll know how to use the information to stay focused and handle the challenge. Living in the optimal world, you may be stressed and have to work hard at coping, *but you can also choose to focus on what you care about.*

## Chapter Five

# Step Back: Replacing Reactivity with Self-Regulation

To *step back*, to slow down, activates the frontal lobes. It's how we can send the first signal to our alarms that everything is all right. For instance, when we take showers in the morning, it is easy to ruminate about the day to come or think about the issues in our lives that are unsettled and unsolved. Thinking about the problems can tense up our muscles or cause us to feel the tingling discomfort of stress. It is our alarms causing us to react. Or…

*We can replace reactivity with self-regulation.*

## Open the Door

Stepping back is the essential first way to open the door between neural pathways connecting the alarm and the learning brain. The alarm slams the door closed; it reacts when it thinks we're in danger. When we step back, we open the pathways for information to travel between all the parts of our brain. A regulated brain is one that is calm and in control. It's a state of being where you choose what you think and feel rather than the alarm dictating your experience.

To start to think clearly, you don't have to go on an all-day retreat or change your lifestyle. You can choose, at any moment, to open communication between your learning brain and the alarm. When you do, the part of your brain that knows you're okay (your thinking center) can convey that reassurance to the part that worries you're in danger (your alarm).

The simple goal of SOS is to focus. Focusing begins by clearing the mind of all thoughts, because it is our intrusive and negative thoughts that produce the alarm reactivity. The moment the thought of an approaching deadline or contentious conversation enters our minds, the alarm wants us to speed up. It wants to solve the problem right now, and stop any possible threat to the rest of our day. That will be helpful later when we're working hard at our desk or need to pay attention to the person with whom we're having the difficult conversation.

In the present moment we can't turn down the alarm by willing ourselves to stop thinking. Telling ourselves "not to worry" is actually another alarm thought; it's an attempt by the alarm to solve the problem of feeling stressed, which makes us even more stressed. Instead, the first part of focusing is one thought, such as, "I am going to pause and slow down." In the shower, as our minds start rushing, all that matters is focusing on the pleasurable feeling of the warm water. It is possible to intentionally just feel the soothing heat and gentle pressure. We can, if we choose to, step back and let our mind be present in what we're experiencing.

Each of us will find different ways to step back. For instance, if you're a person who worries about work, slowing down may be about doing one thing at a time. If you're working with kids in a school or raising a young family, it may be about spending a few minutes just taking a few deep breaths. In the movie *The Matrix*, the main character Neo is introduced by his teacher to the ways he can use his mind to control the imagined world created by the machines. Neo wonders if he will be able to dodge bullets. His teacher, Morpheus, says that when he's ready, he "won't have to." We can't stop bullets in the real world, but we can slow down our reaction to the stressors to the point where our alarms don't continue firing or cause us to melt down.

The first action of SOS is actually to do less. It is to begin letting the learning brain tell the alarm that we recognize what's happening and have it handled. When the brain is in alarm mode, everything is urgent; every situation, whether it really is or not, feels like a problem to solve.

When we step back, we reactivate the learning brain. Instead of feeling the alarms flood, we use our thinking and memory centers to slow the flow of adrenaline and regain the balance of chemicals that allow us to feel calm and in control.

Let's try it again. Right now, something is calling your attention. If you're on a plane, it's the person coughing, making you think you might get sick. The thought of getting sick turns on your alarm. If you're at work, you have so much to do. If you're at home, running a household, you have so much to do. Even if you're on vacation, think of all the things you really should be doing to take advantage of your time off. These days it feels like we always have so much to do.

Does that trigger your alarm? It's so easy for our alarms to get turned on by swirling thoughts and the massive amounts of stimuli surrounding us. Stress is like a roller coaster; slowing down is choosing to step off the ride.

Now close your eyes and take a few deep breaths. How do you feel? If you still feel stressed or tense, take two more slow breaths. Choosing to breathe begins to switch your brain from survival to learning. Just like leaning into the warmth of the shower clears the mind, there is a way, in every situation, for you to begin emptying the alarm thoughts. It is recognizing that your alarm is on and deciding to switch from the chaos of the flood to the calm of focused thinking that makes personal control possible.

## The Truly Focused Mind

The great teachers and performers in every discipline—religion, sports, business—know how to step back. When the world around them is spinning, they know how to remove themselves from the fray. The art of stepping back is as ancient as human civilization itself. Historians of meditation attribute the initial discovery of meditating itself to aboriginal societies spending night after night in front of the fire. Just watching the flickering flame can empty the mind and transport the body to a transcendent place.

The need to step back is a great truth taught by the world's religious traditions. Both the Buddha and Jesus stepped back. Buddha did so by sitting and emptying his mind. Jesus stepped back by going to a quiet place after his teachings and healings. The ascetics of ancient Judaism went to the desert to be away from the chaos of the crowd. The act of Salah in Islam, praying five times a day, begins by placing a prayer rug and facing Mecca. The prayers are an example of orienting to what's most important, but intentionally making space for prayer by laying down the rug is a perfect example of stepping back.

The world of sports offers many good examples. Michael Jordan's pregame routine is a classic. Arguably the greatest basketball player of all time, he says in an interview for one of his sponsors that to mentally prepare for big games,

> I try to relax myself...I listen to music. I joke around with the guys. I take my whole mind away from the game itself. And then when the time comes to focus on the game, I focus on my athletic skills and putting it together with the team; and somehow collectively going out and doing our jobs collectively each and every day. I challenge myself to be the best basketball player every moment that I'm playing the game of basketball.

His idea of taking his "whole mind" away from the game is exactly what it means to step back. The alarm in our brains should react when we're about to play for the championship of the world, but we can notice its message and shift our focus.

In business, there are many ways to step back. Bill Gates took a "think week." Twice each year when he led Microsoft, he would spend a week away reading papers from Microsoft employees. Reading the papers allowed him to orient to what was most important to him, but getting away—that was his way of stepping back. In running one of the leading software firms in the world, where change happens fast and solutions are complex, these times of slowing down were essential in creating his company's success.

Parents may not be able to take a week away from their children, a small-business owner may not have the luxury of stepping back for an extended time without employees to cover, but each of us needs to find ways to intentionally pause. It is the pause that makes focus possible. If we really want to love our kids or be our best selves in the places we work and live, first we need to recognize what our alarm is saying.

## "I Hate to Meditate"

Slowing down does not take days out of your life, or even the traditional twenty minutes recommended by doctors, monks, and yogis for meditation. The twenty minutes is recommended for most people because it takes that long to truly clear our minds. But for many people, traditional meditation doesn't work.

For instance, you sit down in the morning with a simple hope: a few peaceful moments. You know meditating is good for you. Just as trauma and persistent stress change our brains by making the alarm hyperactive, studies show that meditation actually grows the regions of the brain affected by the particular practice. Meditation can make a person more focused or compassionate. Yet, when it comes right down to it, you don't like it. You don't like what happens when you simply sit.

The first problem is the swirling thoughts. They don't stop. The idea of meditating is to focus on breathing, a mantra, or an image. But for some of us, every time we meditate feels like a failure because we can't slow down our minds. Instead of feeling better, our attempts turn up the alarm even further. Our minds aren't quiet; they are a cacophony of competing alarm thoughts screaming for attention.

Meditation isn't for everyone, but each of us needs to find a way to achieve what meditation offers: the clarity that comes when you step back and clear your mind. Even if you've tried every possible form of meditation and none of them seem to work, it's not you that has failed—and it isn't the meditation methods, either. It's that you haven't found the way to step back and clear your mind that works for you. When you do, you'll find that it takes hard work and diligent practice, but you can slow down your mind (we'll give you a list of suggestions in the next section).

The second problem is that if we do actually get to a point where our minds relax a bit, where for just a few seconds we can actually be in the moment, totally focused on the warmth of the sun or a short prayer or mantra, feelings start to pour in—and not the feelings of universal peace and happiness. We start to remember the things we always wanted to do and haven't. We remember past traumas and personal wounds, or current deadlines or things we've forgotten to do. The alarm thoughts that were sitting just below our conscious thought, just waiting for the right time to raise our attention, start to poke us, or worse, cause us incredible anxiety or pain.

People who try meditation and either feel like a failure or experience deep pain don't meditate again. So let's be clear: the first step of SOS is not meditating. It has the same initial goal—clearing the mind. But we're only asking you to be clear for a few moments—at most a few seconds. And you can learn to do this best before you're in high stress situations by taking the time to be present where you are.

Then when you're about to get angry at a member of your family for the same annoying thing they've always done and probably always will do, your brain will remember that you have another option. You can recognize that the nerves you feel before a big presentation are a good thing. You can always recognize stress as your alarm wanting you to be ready for the important moment. That high level of awareness comes from learning to step back.

We believe in the power of meditation, yoga, and taking time away, and we realize that in your busy life you may not be able to do any of these. We realize that in the stress of the modern world you need a strategy you can employ to prepare for times when you feel out of control and in the moments when you're already losing control. The first step to SOS is to open the door to the optimal world. That happens when you sit like Buddha or tell a joke like Michael Jordan. It happens with a breath. It's possible with one simple thought: step back.

# Six Ways to Step Back

We've already invited you to step back by listening and breathing, but we want to make sure you're clear that there is no perfect way to step back. While it would be ideal to have a recipe, opening the door between your alarm and your learning brain is not like making cookies. It may take a different intention in different situations. What is clear is that it is an intention. The first step of SOS is not doing a set of things, but one particular thing; the key is to find the right ways for you. Here are some of the approaches our clients have told us they use to step back successfully.

*Slow Down.* Literally, move slower. If you're walking, reduce your pace. If you're talking, put more space between each word. If you're playing a game, pause in between points, shots, or plays. Once you've read this book, SOS will become a normal part of your life and the simple action of slowing down will begin to turn down your alarm, just as the first taste of chicken soup can immediately make you feel better when you have a cold.

*Mantras.* "Step back" might become your mantra, or another sound, word, or phrase, like "slow down" or "pause." The key is, when you feel your alarm rise, when you recognize the signs that your alarm has taken over your brain, a simple word or phrase can be the reminder that you are in control even when your alarm is firing.

*Breathe.* We're emphasizing it again because there is nothing more cleansing than two intentional breaths. Getting more oxygen in your blood can slow the stress response. Remembering to breathe can activate the learning brain. The great meditators all recommend paying attention to your breath, because when you breathe with purpose, you begin to focus. When you begin to focus, you let your alarm know you're in control.

*Look.* Watch the clouds in the sky. Observe the bird as it builds its nest. Notice the way your child learns to do something new. The simple act of looking places us in the present, begging us to savor the beauty all around us. When alarmed, we can literally fail to see the wonder right in front of us. Looking is a way to step back and enjoy where you are right now.

*Count.* Thomas Jefferson said, "When angry, count to ten. When really angry, count to one hundred." Counting, paying attention to the space between numbers, opens the pathway to the learning brain because you choose to count. The key in any of these approaches is that you choose to do something other than spin through alarm thoughts and emotions that cause you to feel out of control.

*Sweep.* Imagine a chalkboard. On it are horrible thoughts, "You're not good enough." "You can't do this." "What's wrong with you?" Imagine wiping away the thoughts and the board is blank. Imagine a scene in a movie fading to black, or a windshield wiper clearing away the rain. You can, if you choose, sweep your mind blank. When you do, you're ready to switch focus and experience the second letter of SOS.

# Chapter Six

# Orient: Regaining Your Inner Compass

To *orient*, to focus on what's most important to you in this moment, turns down the alarm and strengthens the frontal lobes' ability to think clearly. Think about a moment at work when you wanted to explode. Your body was about to vibrate with overwhelming emotion. Then, you had a thought: "I need this job." Or, "I want to be a good leader." In the next moment, you began to settle down. That is what happens when your thinking center focuses on what is most important to you. Now we're going to teach you how to switch from reactivity—the paralysis of emotional flooding—to focusing.

*You are about to discover your inner compass.*

## Chronic Stress: Lost in an Emotional Flood

When you feel chronically overwhelmed by stress, you live in survival mode; it's like you're running on automatic pilot. You are not in control of your brain or what you feel, think, or do; your brain's alarm is. Your body can switch at the drop of a hat from being calm and relaxed to flooding with emotion. Anger, fear, and worry can erupt like a volcano and rush through your veins, leaving you a wreck—and often what you do next can hurt you and the people around you. Stress reactions are not mild wake-up calls, but instead can feel like you're being spun under water in powerful waves of physical and emotional distress.

Emotional flooding is what's happening at those moments, or on those entire days or weeks when your life feels completely out of control. The flood is not a sign that you're losing your mind or coming completely unglued. When this happens, and it can and does happen to *every* human being sooner or later, you've been swept away, even if only temporarily, by a flood of alarm signals. You need to regain your bearings. This happens when you focus on one thought.

## Nearly Naked

When June heard the click, she panicked. She'd just walked out her front door onto the porch to put a birthday card to her niece in the mailbox. She didn't want to forget as she rushed off to work in the morning, and she'd remembered to do it right before bed. The problem now was that she was outside in underwear and a T-shirt on a cool fall night and the door behind her was locked.

She didn't have an extra key. Her neighbors who did were gone. Her windows were all closed to keep the house warm. She literally felt her alarm kick in. Her body started to sweat, even though she was cold and barely clothed. Her thoughts started to spin: there was no way she could go walking down the street in her underwear. What was she going to do?

When she described this story to us, what she explained next is exactly how the learning brain can send the signal to the alarm that everything is under control. She heard her Grandma's voice. Now on first reading, that sounds crazy. She's locked outside of her house and she hears the ghost of her grandmother. But she didn't hear a ghost; her learning brain accessed a file of a voice she would trust.

She had been through a course on SOS, so she was familiar with what she needed to do in times of stress and she'd practiced many times. Her grandma's voice said, "Step back." She didn't listen the first time. She was overwhelmed with thoughts about all she had to do the next day, being outside alone in the dark with no clothes, and how she really wanted to go to Hawaii at least once before she died. That's the way the alarm works: it hijacks the brain and suddenly a simple mistake becomes a flood of thoughts and emotions that tap into every fear, doubt, and worry we've ever had.

She heard her grandma's voice again, "Stop and think." This time she listened. She closed her eyes and took a few deep breaths, paying attention to the sounds of the air flowing in and out. Then she oriented to what was most important to her in her life at that moment: the love and wisdom of her grandmother.

The weight of fear and embarrassment fell off her shoulders. She wasn't relaxed and wholly at peace—she was still standing in front of her house in her underwear. But she felt a sense of calm and confidence because she had her grandmother's love to help her feel safe in a helpless moment. What had been anxiety and shame transformed into determination and good humor.

She looked at the locked door. She looked to her left at the neighbor's house, then to her right at the tree in her front yard, and she remembered: the towel. Orienting allowed her learning brain to remember. She had put a towel out on her back deck to dry after going to the beach that day. She hadn't brought it inside yet. Never had she worn a more fashionable skirt as she went to get help.

## The Orienting Response

When animals and human beings sense something unexpected or unfamiliar, our reptile and emotional brains tend to trigger an automatic reaction. The body's sensory and perceptual organs redirect—or reorient—their focus toward the source or trigger. This orienting response seems to serve a survival function because what we don't understand or recognize as familiar may be dangerous. Not surprisingly, this reflexive, automatic orienting doesn't involve the brain's thinking center. It can provide new information that may be extremely helpful in terms of protecting our safety, but it doesn't lead to new learning.

We're about to teach you to engage a similar but much more powerful orienting response. The part of your brain that gets shut down during an extreme stress reaction—your thinking center—can be reactivated by orienting your mind to the greatest source of strength and power that any human being can tap into: the thoughts that give you hope and make life worth living.

Regaining orientation—your sense of perspective about what's really important in your life—is exactly what's needed to find your way out of the confusion that unbridled stress reactions cause. You know that, but in the middle of a prolonged or intense stress reaction it's easy to forget what's important. The immediate pressures and crises seem to demand all of your attention. Now it's time to translate what we all know—that there are countless opportunities every day to make course corrections that can make the difference between success and failure—into action.

Every time you step back from the immediate pressures and pleasures of life is a chance to not only regroup and rejuvenate, but also to reorient. When you reorient, you gain personal control no matter what external circumstances you face. That's because the act of orienting activates your thinking center, and empowers your thinking center to be an equal partner to your alarm. Ultimately, that resets your brain's alarm.

There are so many ways to think. You can imagine or pull images from your memory center. You can construct words or phrases. You can visualize, literally seeing something that hasn't happened yet, or pull files from memory that play back like video. You can feel the emotions that you want experience. You can reflect on what values will guide your life. You can dream about your goals. Each of these are a form of thinking, but to orient is to focus your whole mind solely on one powerful thought: whatever is most important to you in your life right at this moment.

## Just Drive

It is possible in every moment to stay focused on a thought that sends the message to the alarm that there is nothing to worry about, even when you've just been cut off in traffic. As we described in chapter two, the moment a person cuts us off, our alarms should fire. Whether we have to swerve or slam on the brakes, it is the alarm, even if we don't realize it's forcing us to act, that makes unconscious action possible. A learning brain that's functioning optimally takes advantage of the alarm signals to make sure we're safe, then calmly returns our attention to the road—but that's not always the way it works.

The problem is the next moment.

When our bodies fill with adrenaline, we get angry. We often shake our fists and yell. There is no gesture in the world more clear than what most drivers extend after being cut off. And the anger and righteousness doesn't help. It doesn't make us better drivers. It doesn't make the roads safer. The person who cut us off may have been talking on his cell phone, but he also may have been distracted by his child in the back seat or he may have made the simple mistake of not checking his blind spot.

The answer: just drive.

If we really want to make the world a better place, imagine if, when cut off in traffic, all drivers stepped back and reoriented to enjoying the drive. This is not an attempt to make you a weakling on the road. This is about your mental, emotional, and physical health. It's about making you the kind of person who knows what's really worth an alarm reaction and what's best handled with an SOS.

To *just drive* is to hold the steering wheel and enjoy the feel of controlling a two-ton vehicle. It's listening to the sound of the road and the hum of the engine. It's opening the window and feeling the wind on your face. It's focusing on what you're heading toward that matters to you. To orient your senses on just driving, rather than hating anonymous fellow travelers who may themselves be having an overactive alarm reaction, means you feel calm and enjoy the moment. The people with you in the car and sharing the road will see the peace and pleasure on your face.

# Why Bother to Orient? The Costs of Mindfulness

We spend considerable time in our own heads, haunted by the past or worrying about the future. We lose track of what we really care about. We drift through our lives in a daze, or rush forward without giving more than a fleeting thought to where we're headed. And we don't even realize it...until we melt down.

Then, often as we're about to hurtle over a cliff that's partially of our own making, or find ourselves trapped on a path that it's too late to reverse, we have those poignant, tragic moments of insight. Like sleepers awakening from a nightmare, we can see it all clearly. But even at times of apparently unavoidable disaster, it may not be too late. Even more importantly, every day is filled with opportunities to avert disasters before they happen and focus on what matters most.

*To orient is exactly that: a conscious, mindful return to what's most important in our lives.* So why don't we orient to what's most important in our lives in every moment? Why do we need research studies and books to teach us how to use our brains more effectively?

*Lack of awareness* is the major barrier to orienting. We don't recognize that while we're busy using our minds to sort through what our senses tell us, we use this information to do the bidding of the alarm without paying attention to the thinking center. We constantly use our minds to think, but we do so using only a fraction of the brainpower at our disposal. By failing to purposefully activate the thinking center we lose out on their invaluable input—and we give free rein to our alarm to run our thinking and our lives. This is like leaving the most immature members of a family in charge: there will be a lot of excitement but also a lot of crises without enough consideration of what's really important.

*Habit* is a second key barrier to orienting. We think reflecting on our purpose in life or contemplating our core values is a frivolous waste of time, or we're too busy. Then we get in the habit of only paying attention to the trouble and problems we face, and we ignore the things we really want and need. That's fine most of the time, because it satisfies the needs of the alarm and reward centers, but leaves the thinking center mindlessly filling the alarm's requests.

*Effort* is a third barrier to orienting. Scientific studies that directly observe the brain through tools such as functional magnetic resonance imaging (fMRI) have shown that it takes more chemical and electrical activation in the brain—translation: effort—to focus the mind on complex thoughts such as values and goals than to simply allow the brain to go on automatic pilot. When you actually think about what something means, that takes more brainpower than simply thinking about the thing itself or even how to get it (if it's a reward) or avoid it (if it's trouble).

A fourth barrier to orienting is related to effort: *speed*. It's much quicker to simply react than to actually think. In fact, brain scientists have identified two distinct pathways in the brain that stress activates. The first pathway is called the "short" or "fast" loop because it literally is a circle that involves a small amount of physical terrain in the brain and rapid signals in a small number of brain cells (neurons). It begins with input from areas that analyze sensory information, which are positioned near and report directly to the amygdala, and alarm instructions to the reptilian brain from the amygdala to speed up or slow down body functions such as heart rate or breathing. These result in feedback to close the loop from the activated body areas to the sensory processors in the brain.

## Activate the Long Loop

The alternate pathway is what scientist Joseph LeDoux calls the "long" or "slow" loop because it covers more territory in the brain and takes longer. The major difference is that this loop includes the brain's thinking center in addition to all of the other brain areas in the short/fast loop. This takes longer because the thinking center is located further from the alarm and lower brain areas and a larger number of neurons must be activated to send its more complex messages back to those areas. No surprise really: actually thinking takes longer (and more effort) than simply reacting.

With all these barriers or potential disadvantages, why bother to think deeply, or even to think at all? The obvious answer is that mindful choices are usually better in the long run than mindless reactions. But that's never been reason enough to deter most of us from choosing ease and efficiency over effort. We need a better reason than merely the value of making wise rather than impulsive decisions to justify the cost in energy and time required to use our thinking centers more than occasionally.

Surprisingly, it is the alarm that comes to the rescue of the thinking center, if we understand how those two areas of the brain actually work together. You'd think that the alarm would be all about immediate survival and rewards. But actually, that's what the alarm gets hooked on, like an addict, when it doesn't get what really meets its needs. The most powerful reward and reassurance for the alarm is not a stress reaction; that's just what it will settle for if it can't get its true needs met.

The alarm really wants us to focus on what nourishes and satisfies the thinking center. Just like the proverbial toddler, the alarm needs help in resetting itself when it gets frantic, shuts down our body, or revs up our emotions. And just like a parent with a toddler, the thinking center has to be creative, patient, and persistent in order to calm down a fractious alarm (for example, when you're feeling overwhelmed by anxiety or anger) or wake up a shut-down alarm (for example, when you're feeling so discouraged or exhausted that you don't care anymore and want to just give up).

This may sound like a lot of extra work for our brains, in particular for the thinking center, but the payoff can be phenomenal. It is just like the satisfaction that parents feel when their toddler is able to calm down after being upset. It's the feeling of relief. One of the most pleasurable human experiences is the joy that occurs when your brain's alarm gets reset. And it's not one of those fleeting pleasures that are quickly followed by a letdown.

After the alarm is reset it takes a while, and usually a good deal of stress, for it to go back into survival mode. That's because the most natural mode for the alarm is the optimum scenario in which it's partnering with—rather than dictating to, or attempting to do the job of—the think-ing center. It is the need and natural tendency of the brain's alarm to be mentored by the thinking center, which gives us the greatest incentive to make the effort of activating our learning brains. The payoff is a happy and cooperative alarm, which is the definition of well-managed stress.

## An Oriented Life

Henry David Thoreau moved to a little one-room cabin near Walden Pond on July 4, 1945. In the years previous he had been frustrated. He worked as a tutor, editorial assistant, and repairman in the house of Ralph Waldo Emerson, the famous writer and lecturer. But Thoreau wanted to write. He was in his mid-twenties, restless, and wanted to live outside of what he considered the "over-civilization" of the surrounding areas.

So he built a house on land owned by Emerson at the urging of a fellow poet. His entire life became an SOS. He stated his purpose clearly in *Walden*, his book about the two-year experiment in simple living.

> *I went to the woods because I wished to live deliberately, to front only the essential facts of life, and see if I could not learn what it had to teach, and not, when I came to die, discover that I had not lived. I did not wish to live what was not life, living is so dear; nor did I wish to practice resignation, unless it was quite necessary. I wanted to live deep and suck out all the marrow of life, to live so sturdily and Spartan-like as to put to rout all that was not life, to cut a broad swath and shave close, to drive life into a corner, and reduce it to its lowest terms, and, if it proved to be mean, why then to get the whole and genuine meanness of it, and publish its meanness to the world; or if it were sublime, to know it by experience, and be able to give a true account of it in my next excursion.*

There may never be a greater example of constant and intentional orient-ing. His alarm told him that there was more to life and a different way to learn than living with the Emersons.

He literally stepped back, two miles into the woods, and focused each day on what mattered most to him. He wanted to "live deliberately." So he grew his own food, and farmed a 2.5-acre bean field that funded his time away.

Every day, Thoreau made a point of focusing on the natural environment around him. He saw and heard things he'd always overlooked. He found in Walden Pond a universe of ideas about how to live. He wasn't hiding from the world. When he heard the sounds of modern civilization, for example the train's whistle at Concord Station, he was angry because he wanted to hear only the tree frogs and the birds. But he noticed his alarm and refocused on his surroundings because to him, nothing was more important than just seeing and hearing and being fully aware of the natural world.

Thoreau went into the woods to write. But we'd say that, even more so, he went to find what was important enough to him to be worth writing about. While he would revise the book *Walden* over the next ten years, he wrote first about his experience—what he observed when he stepped back from his ordinary life—every day of the two years, two months, and two days he lived in the woods. And his learning brain stayed active for at least another eight years, long enough to create a masterpiece of simplicity and insight.

Walden was the most productive period of his writing career. Imagine the pleasure: focusing only on the craft that matters most to you. By immersing himself in his work and in the beauty of his surroundings, Thoreau was able to step back and orient himself. During the rest of his life, as he fought against slavery and for the preservation of the natural world, he found strength by drawing on that ability to focus on what was most important to him.

## Stepping Off the Roller Coaster

Orienting means we choose to focus on what truly matters to us instead of living distracted. The high-speed roller coaster of modern life—modern technology, virtual reality, and social networking—is not wrong; it takes us for a ride that constantly activates our alarms, and that's not wrong either. What's wrong is that most of us never realize that the alarm is running our lives.

After making the decision to step back and ground yourself in the present moment, you have to have something practical to do in order to focus and feel better. Here's how you can start the process of orienting to what you really value (we'll go through more specific ways to orient in part three). Take a few minutes and come up with a personal list of what's most important to you. Consider the following:

- People like family, friends, role models, and mentors (animals count too)
- Places you've been and loved
- Places you dream of visiting
- Activities you love to do and look forward to
- Beliefs about what is good in life
- Moments that you've most treasured
- Values about how the world should be
- Goals, both for personal achievement and making the world a better place

Now take this list and circle four or five items that mean the most to you in terms of giving you a feeling that your life has been and can continue to be fulfilling and worth living.

This can be difficult to do if you're under considerable stress right now, or if you're recovering from a previous stressful experience and still feeling the physical and emotional burden. Again, this is your alarm in control. If the alarm in your brain is telling you that nothing really matters, or nothing important really lasts or can be counted on, that's a signal that your thinking center may need some help or support to get turned on again.

Support might come simply from being with people whom you know you can trust and who care about you, or from a therapist or counselor or spiritual leader. With the patience and support of someone who loans you his or her learning brain, it's possible to step back from the pressure and stress just enough to begin the process of orienting yourself to what's important.

On the other hand, you may have found it very easy and even enjoyable to take the time to focus very specifically on who and what gives you the greatest sense of fulfillment and meaning. Having done that, you might think that you're done—that making the list is the solution. This is just the beginning. The solution is focusing on these sources of meaning.

The next step is to take your short list of key people, places, activities, goals, and values, and put it into action. That means finding times every day when you step back from the immediate rush and take a few moments to focus your mind on one item from that list. Each time you focus on *one thought that you choose*, you create a safe space in your mind that is free of all distractions. You tell your alarm that you're in control. It's like having an empty bank vault, and you're starting to fill it with what's precious to you. Your memory center won't forget.

Every time you do this, you teach your brain and your mind to orient. Like any new skill, it may seem hard at first. But when people learn to orient, we hear them say things like,

"When I let myself become focused entirely on my partner, the racing thoughts slow down."

"My worries and frustrations don't bother me as much and they actually do go away if I keep focusing on one thought."

"I realized that alarm reactions were hiding my true feelings, and when I oriented to the people and values that I care most about, I actually could feel some genuine hope and love again."

Learning to orient doesn't mean, at first, that you can instantly recover from a body and brain flooded with the chemicals of stress. But with dedicated practice, orienting can change the way you experience each day without needing to double or triple your income or change any of the people, places, or activities in your life. Orienting strengthens the thinking center's ability to help you think clearly, and that's worth a lot even when life is stress free.

And orienting can prepare the thinking center to partner with, and guide, the alarm when you're dealing with stress or even in the middle of a full-scale meltdown. The stepping back and orienting portions of SOS can provide that small but invaluable pause that keeps us from reacting. It shows us that even if we're in incredible pain or distress, we can still choose how we use the amazing resource that we have in our brains. That can be the key to changing how we handle stressful events and their outcomes. When you've mastered the first two steps of SOS, you'll know you can handle even the most difficult moments of life, and day by day, you'll have fewer stress meltdowns. In fact, when you have discovered your inner compass, you'll feel less stress day to day.

Like stepping back, there is no perfect way to orient that will work for every situation or perfectly turn down or reset your alarm. The more you step back and orient, the stronger the neural pathway in your brain will become, helping you remember that you've been stressed before and can handle it. Every time you remind your alarm you're in control, it slows the flow of adrenaline to your body and raises your learning brain's ability to feel in control. But sometimes the first thing we focus on doesn't calm us down or help us raise our level of control. That's why we have to self-check.

# Chapter Seven

# Self-Check: Reading Your Body's Dashboard

To *self-check* is to notice the functioning of our alarms and thinking centers so we fill our memories with files that keep us safe and allow us to focus on what's most important. Our fundamental natures begin like animals. Scared dogs cower or bark. A stressed-out horse will start sweating or bucking. An angry lion roars. Like these animals, when people feel stressed, we react.

When human beings are stressed, we go through the same physiological and emotional changes—shaking, sweating, heightened heart rate, feeling frightened, angry, or depressed—like any other animal. But much, if not most of the time, we don't pay attention to these stress reactions; we only notice them when we can no longer ignore them. When we don't pay attention to the feelings of our bodies or emotional lives, we lose huge amounts of valuable information.

Whether you realize it or not, *your brain can read your body like a dashboard.*

## Transcending the Inner Ostrich

Stress-related feelings usually aren't very pleasant, but like an ostrich burying its head in the sand, what you don't know about what you're feeling can hurt you. Stress-related physical and emotional feelings are a signal from your brain's alarm that you need to pay attention to something that's an actual or potential problem or danger. If you don't pay attention to the feelings, you probably won't notice the problem or danger—until it's too late.

We've already talked about the important pitfall of not paying attention to your alarm, but it's important to emphasize it one more time as we finish introducing you to SOS: feelings caused by stress reactions don't go away if we ignore them, any more than a predator goes away when the ostrich buries its head. In the modern world, the problem with stress-related feelings usually is not a predator that's about to attack us. The problem is that the alarm will continue to signal, or even escalate its stress signal, if we don't pay attention to its message.

At the same time, paying attention to stress-related feelings does not mean dwelling on them and making yourself miserable. This kind of rumination, in fact, is exactly what happens when we try to ignore those feelings, and the alarm ups the ante when it's not being heard. Animals react; as human beings, we have the capacity to choose what we do with the information our bodies provide. When you feel stressed and get anxious, angry, or depressed, you can lash out or you can crawl into a corner. Or, you can be the person who recognizes the emotion as it happens, does an SOS, and then responds in a way that is most appropriate to what you want to achieve or experience in a given moment.

Instead of being an ostrich, when you name what your body and emotions feel like, you activate your brain's thinking center. By doing this you enable the thinking center to signal your brain's alarm that you're taking its call to action seriously. Bringing the thinking center online also provides the necessary support to help the alarm play its role without trying to run the whole show. By simply paying attention to specific bodily and emotional feelings, you provide the alarm with a partner to help it develop an optimum solution to the problem it senses instead of relying on a survival reaction that is unlikely to be effective except in rare cases of extreme danger.

Just as we have the choice to step back and choose to orient when we need to focus our mind and handle stressful experiences, we also have the choice to take our emotional pulse.

## Discovering Your Brain's Dashboard

Your body as well as your emotions provide your brain with a virtual dashboard. The concept of a dashboard began with automobiles and pilots whose operators needed to ensure the vehicle's many complicated systems worked properly. The visual experience of dashboards in machines has been greatly simplified by computers and the user interfaces that easily allow an operator to flow between different readouts. Even businesses now use dashboards to keep track of their data—whether related to production, finance, or performance. With new technology like tablets and smart phones, it's easy to monitor large quantities of information and make it accessible.

Unfortunately, there is no automated or high-definition dashboard for the human body and mind (not yet, at least). If we know how to use it, however, we have a virtual dashboard that is every bit as informative. Consider the levels of your brain again. The reptile brain keeps track of our basic needs like food, rest, and air. Our emotional brain tracks essential moment-to-moment conditions like how alert we need to be and how much pleasure we're experiencing. The thinking center can notice the signals from the lower levels of the brain in every instant. It is this feedback, captured by the learning brain from the body and emotions, that is your virtual dashboard.

Stress reactions are actually a combination of many emotions. They are the feelings that are organized and orchestrated (via the reptile brain and the body's nervous system) primarily by the brain's alarm. We give these specific feelings names like fear, worry, anxiety, and anger. If we pay attention, our thinking centers can get almost constant readouts of our bodies' stress reaction and stress management systems, which are like the accelerator and braking systems in a car.

Heart rate, muscle tension, and breathing rate each serve as a speedometer-like readout of how stressed we are. Every emotion can also tell you something vital about how your life is going. Although we often think of emotions as noise that distracts from more important thoughts or that interfere with efficient decision making and action, nothing could be further from the truth.

Research studies repeatedly demonstrate that when people recognize and objectively describe these stress feelings, this alone tends to reduce the severity or distress caused by the feelings. Naming the stress feeling and describing how intense or discomforting it is (as we're suggesting you to do on a scale of one to ten) actually doesn't make the stress feeling go away, but does increase our confidence that we know what we're dealing with and can handle it.

Why does this simple act of naming the feeling and its intensity change how you feel? One of the reasons is that checking that virtual dashboard and thinking about its readout involves the brain's thinking center. Doing this intentionally focuses the mind on learning something that may be helpful, rather than a stress reaction that is dictated by the alarm. The alarm doesn't care what stress you're feeling or how much, it just wants you to wake up and do something so you'll survive. But by checking the emotional dashboard for your stress level, you've shown your alarm that you are alert and taking action, which is the message that turns down the alarm. The simple act of doing a self-check is an act of learning, and perhaps the most meaningful learning to your brain: you're learning about you and what you care about most.

## The Stress Thermometer

Let's actually do the third step of SOS, *self-check*, as we did at the beginning of the first chapter. Slowly, intentionally, we're having you practice this way of living so you both understand how it impacts the brain and feel the difference it makes in your body and emotions.

Just like placing two fingers to your neck and feeling for the beat of your heart, you can, at any moment, check your level of stress and the emotions stress induces. You can also check the amount of personal control you feel you have. Let's start with stress, and its related emotions; then we'll finish the chapter focusing on personal control.

The stress we're referring to is not the challenges and irritations you deal with in the world of work, school, and family. We mean the feeling of stress chemicals that flow through your body when something triggers your alarm.

On a scale of one to ten, with one being the lowest and ten being the highest you've ever experienced, rate your level of stress right now. Remember, stress is neither good nor bad; it is simply the alarm sending chemicals through your body because something needs your attention.

The reason the thermometer starts with a one rather than zero is that our alarms are never "off." If your alarm were at a zero, you'd be underground. You don't want your alarm to be inactive because then it can't respond to keep you safe. If you're sitting outside reading, and suddenly the clouds turn ominously black, you want to notice. Right now, hopefully your alarm is sending low intensity signals because you're enjoying this book and your memory center is productively activated, creating helpful new files of this content and the pleasure of learning.

You want to measure your stress level because you want to recognize when your thinking center is productively activated as well (which turns down the alarm even further because when you want to learn more, the alarm knows there's nothing to worry about). If you're totally stress free, at a level one, you feel calm and alert; you still notice your surroundings, but you feel as little stress as you've ever felt. When you think about things that have been stressful in the past, they pass through your mind like you're the Buddha sitting under a tree. Your body has little or no tension—your shoulders are relaxed and you're free of any headache or muscle pain.

Think about what you just learned. You can feel and notice the moments when your body is completely at ease. Notice this moment, whether you feel totally stress free or not, because the entirety of part three is about giving you the power to focus on the ways of orienting that allow you to feel stress free by choice more often than you ever thought possible.

But your alarm also might be at a two or a three right now. If your alarm is sending some distinct but relatively mild signals that you need to pay attention—perhaps to keep you awake if you're feeling sleepy, or maybe to remind you, gently but firmly, to use your memory center so you can remember this content to tell a friend or teach someone at work tomorrow—you're not completely relaxed.

It also would be perfectly normal if you were having a moderately strong stress reaction right at this moment. You might rate your stress level as a five, six, or seven in this case. Either because of something you've read in this book or something going on in your life that may have no relationship to what you're reading, your alarm is sending stress chemicals through your body. It's entirely possible to read and learn while having a moderate stress reaction. That just means that your alarm is signaling you to pay attention to something, and your thinking center is balancing that input by helping you keep focus on what you're reading.

Experiencing a total stress meltdown while you're reading is unlikely. You're focused on the page, oriented to what's most important to you as your thinking center learns from the words before you and your memory center files your conclusions.

But if something serious has happened recently or you anticipate a stressful event which requires your full and careful attention, then asking you to measure your stress level might have triggered a pre-crisis mobilization signal from your alarm. This stress reaction is higher than if you hadn't thought of an upcoming challenge. That doesn't necessarily mean that anything is wrong with you or with your life. It's a wake-up call from your alarm, reminding you to prepare in advance rather than waiting to the last moment, or not to get blindsided by a stressor you've forgotten.

Suggesting that you could be having a stress reaction could, in fact, trigger a stress reaction. You could suddenly be feeling strong emotions, like anger, guilt, or anxiety. Racing thoughts could flood your mind. Your body could tense up like a rubber band pulled taut. You might feel trapped in a troubling state of increasingly unmanageable stress. If that happened to you just now, you might be getting to a near-peak stress level, as high as a nine—although that level usually should be reserved for a major challenge or threat that demands immediate action, like a car accident or your child running out into traffic.

A level ten meltdown fortunately is rare. It might feel like the world is coming to an end or even that life is not worth living. This can happen either because of a truly life-altering or life-threatening event, or because of a breakdown in brain chemistry that leads to serious psychiatric illness and symptoms, such as wanting to take your own life. It can happen even when there really is no such extreme emergency, because we're worn down or exhausted physically or emotionally. When we're overwhelmed, what might otherwise seem like a six, seven, or at most eight on the stress thermometer might escalate into a full-scale meltdown simply because our alarms are out of alignment with the real level of threat.

Make no mistake though, if you're sure that your or someone else's stress level is a ten, if a self-check reveals this really is the worst stress you or another has ever felt, it's time to get immediate help. That's what paramedics, hospital emergency departments, and emergency hotlines are for. It's always better to err on the side of being safe. Thankfully, we rarely experience the highest levels of stress, even in the middle of very stressful lives. Hopefully, even if your alarm might have risen as we asked you to think about it, you can reorient to enjoying these pages and return it to a low and pleasantly attentive state.

Measuring our stress levels is important because we need to know when we should feel stress and when our brains overreact. A person who melts down on vacation after working exceptionally hard for months or even years, for instance, might have ignored her alarm for weeks on end because of what she felt she had to do. Then, when the waiter brings the wrong meal at dinner, her alarm sends a signal of nine or ten, though it really should only send out a four or a five. Measuring stress all along the way allows a person to catch the false alarm and refocus on what matters—in this case, enjoying time away and a pleasant meal.

When you develop a knack for reading your body's dashboard,

extreme stress reactions tend to occur less often because the problems, dangers, and challenges that can culminate in an emergency get recognized and dealt with earlier, when stress levels are still mild. As human beings, when we read our bodies as dashboards and notice the signals our brains send in the form of emotions, we can then use the information to reach the goals and create the level of stress we need to live the lives we want.

## The Value of Stress

Have you ever heard an athlete say, "I was flat out there today"? It's because they weren't focused. When you're having a bad day and just can't get your mind on your work, it can be because your alarm is too low. The power of measuring your stress level is that you can notice both when it's too high and when it's too low. Two examples help make the point: endurance athletics and public presentations.

Most marathoners struggle before their first 26.2-mile race. Even if they have trained properly, the anxiety about completing the extraordinary distance can sap the energy and focus they need to complete the event. Long-distance athletes who know how to measure and manage their alarms, however, can use the energy from their stress response to optimize what their bodies can produce.

Famed marathoner Grete Waitz did intuitively what you can do using SOS. Recognizing her decade-long track career and short-distance world championships, organizers of the 1978 New York City Marathon invited Waitz to participate. Many of the elite marathons hire a "rabbit," a fast runner to set the pace for the other competitors in hopes of generating faster times among the leaders. Rabbits rarely finish the whole race. Waitz, however, did much more than just show up and run a few fast miles at the start.

She and her husband treated the trip to New York as a second honeymoon. Not only was she calm the night before, she celebrated. They had a four-course meal with steak, wine, and ice cream. She started the race with thirteen thousand other runners and ran fast and comfortable for nineteen miles. Then she did the same thing you can do with SOS.

She took notice as her body started to break down. Her brain struggled too, because as a European who was used to thinking in terms of the metric system, she didn't know how to convert miles into meters. She literally didn't know how much farther she had to run. This could have entirely sapped her energy, but instead, she focused on one idea.

She wrote about the day in the book *First Marathons*:

> *I began to get annoyed and frustrated. Every time I saw a patch of trees, I thought, "Oh, this must be Central Park," but no. To keep motivated, I started swearing at my husband for getting me into this mess in the first place.*

It's funny to think about, but as she got tired, focusing on her husband increased her sense of personal control and that lowered her alarm to a level in which she could pump adrenaline in just the right amount to keep going strong. If she had stayed at a stress level of eight, nine, or even ten, frustrated or panicked about completing the race, she might not have finished. Her final result: first place and a new world record.

Waitz's body was incredibly strong, but it was her brain—and specifically, her ability to orient herself to the one thing that was most important in her life at that moment—that gave her the strength to triumph.

Don't be confused by the way she tells the story, either. You might think that she powered herself to a victory and the record using anger as her fuel. But if she'd merely been angry, simply reacting to the stress she felt as confusion and exhaustion triggered her alarm, she wouldn't have succeeded. It was her ability to mentally channel her stress reaction, anger and all, by focusing on the person that meant the world to her, which raised her to another level physically and mentally.

When we pay attention to the signals from our brains' alarms on a regular basis, we then have the ability to take the next step and choose to focus on something that will raise our stress level or lower it depending on the level of arousal we need in a given situation.

Public speaking is another example of when too much alarm causes us to be nervous and block our learning brain, but when there is not enough, we are flat.

On a trip to Australia in June of 2011, the Dalai Lama, spiritual leader of Tibet, held a press conference. The prime minister, Julia Gillard, chose not to meet with him, and when asked whether he was disappointed, he replied, no. "If your prime minister has some kind of spiritual interest then of course my meeting would be useful," he told reporters at Parliament House. "Otherwise, I have nothing to ask him. Also, you see, there's no point to seek advice from him."

When his advisors whispered that the prime minister is a woman, he quickly corrected himself. "Oh, from her."

In the video, the audience laughs. The Dalai Lama doesn't miss a beat. A normal person making such a mistake in public might immediately have a stress response. He might fumble over words, turn red, or try to justify the mistake. But the Dalai Lama simply corrected his error and continued.

In his regular meditation practice, as a person who has given thousands of talks and interviews all over the world, the Dalai Lama intuitively knows how to measure his stress. He has gained such a high level of personal control that mistakes don't bother him when his focus is on communicating his message. Every person, in his or her own style, is capable of self-checking stress to feel in control, even in difficult situations.

## An Alternative Stress Thermometer: Your Anger Level

The general stress thermometer works for most people to measure and manage their stress levels. There may, however, also be a more specific emotion you can use depending on your life and the places you continue to have heightened alarm reactions. The goal of measuring stress is to train your mind to notice the rise and fall of your alarm signals, so you can switch focus to what's most important in a given moment. If stress in general feels like too broad a measure, or if you have experienced specific forms of hyperactive alarm reactions, such as intense anxiety or nervousness, you can self-check these signals from your emotional brain.

One of the emotions our clients have also found valuable to self-check is anger. After being ordered by a judge to return to an anger management class for the sixth time, a client of one of our colleagues said, "I know plenty of anger management skills, and when I use them I can handle anger fine. It's just that the only time my anger management skills don't work is when I'm too angry to remember to use them!"

Anger is a classic stress reaction that originates in signals from the brain's alarm. Anger rarely feels good, but it doesn't have to lead to bad outcomes. The problem for most people is we forget to use our anger management skills as we start to get angry.

Measuring anger can be important even for the most trained stress reducers. The National Public Radio talk show *Car Talk* received a fascinating call from a woman named Joyce. Her husband suffered from road rage. While normally the show offers advice on how to fix cars, she wanted advice on how to fix her husband. She described him behind the wheel as a human cross between champion race-car driver Mario Andretti and Tony Soprano, famed Mob boss on the HBO hit show *The Sopranos*. The twist: her husband was a meditation teacher.

No amount of time doing traditional forms of stress reduction will work if you don't know how to pay attention to your alarm and how to focus on the emotions it sends you. That doesn't mean getting hung up or trapped in upsetting emotions. To focus on unpleasant feelings is not the same as ruminating or obsessing. Focusing is observing and finding meaning and value, just as Thoreau did in nature. Emotions are much like the world of nature, often harsh and ugly at first glance, but ultimately a guide to deeper understanding.

Although it's not a complete solution, simply paying attention to anger can be the best way to prevent the chronic buildup of angry feelings or the explosive rage that can happen when our brains melt down. Similar to doing a stress self-check, doing an anger self-check is best learned and practiced when you're *not* feeling angry. Obviously, it's difficult to stop and think clearly enough to rate your anger level when you're really frustrated or outraged. However, if you've diligently practiced checking-in on anger with your body and emotions at times when you're not feeling angry at all, the skill can kick in almost automatically. And that brief moment of self-check can make a crucial difference between letting anger control you versus feeling angry but being in control.

Doing anger self-checks when you're not angry prepares you to do the self-check when you are angry, and it builds a greater degree of trust on the part of the alarm, showing it that the thinking center can be counted on to be alert without constant reminders when small triggers occur.

An additional benefit of doing an anger self-check when you're not angry is that you may actually *be* angry and not know it. When done carefully, the anger self-check is an opportunity to detect early signs of anger that might otherwise be missed. When you discover anger unexpectedly, it usually is not extreme and can be dealt with immediately. Then you know what your alarm is telling you, and your thinking center can develop a plan to handle the situation in a thoughtful and proactive manner before anger becomes rage.

Right now, on a scale of one to ten, with one being the lowest and ten being the highest you've ever experienced, rate your level of anger. Remember, like stress, anger is neither good nor bad; it is simply the alarm sending chemicals through your body because something needs your attention.

If your anger level is very low, a three or less, that's good to know. Whether you realized it or not, you pay attention to your alarm and use your thinking center to handle situations in your life effectively. A low anger level is a sign either that your life is relatively free of irritations, or (more often) that in spite of the ordinary frustrations (or even serious problems) that are common in all of our lives, your thinking center has partnered with your alarm to deal with things before your anger becomes severe.

If your anger level is mid-range, say between four and six, these are early warning signals from your alarm that you need to pay attention to something that is becoming, or has become, a problem. Don't rush to any conclusions, but take this as an opportunity to think about situations, people, and other potential sources of frustration that may need attention. This anger level is an opportunity for prevention or a reminder to start tracking situations that may need prevention.

Less often, but importantly, you may identify a strong sense of anger, in the seven to nine range. This almost always is due to messages from your alarm demanding that you do something. Even at a high level of anger, however, recognizing the seriousness of the situation places you in a better position to act thoughtfully (with input from your thinking center, rather than just on impulse) and effectively.

And of course, if your anger rating is at the maximum, a ten, it is essential to do something to correct the problem or deal with the danger. If this is happening as you read this book, it's because we've triggered a memory from your past or raised your awareness of a situation you've been ignoring. Anger at this level is best handled if you have an emergency plan already in place to prevent your alarm from pushing you to explode or shut down and give up. The best plan always is highly individual—based on what's best for you as a person, and what is best for the specific situation(s) in question.

An effective plan for dealing with a ten on the anger scale, however, usually involves teaming up with other people you trust to set right something that has gone seriously wrong. In turning peak anger events into successfully solved problems, it's particularly important not to isolate yourself from support and help.

As with stress and anger, the thermometer can be used with any emotion you're experiencing: addiction urges, frustration, anxiety, or worry.

In each case, when you notice the physical and emotional signs of the feeling with your thinking center, you train your alarm to reduce the amount of stress chemicals it releases into your body.

## Stress Awareness Makes Stress Reduction Possible

Nowhere is it more important to recognize your level of stress than in personal relationships. When Carrie and Tom came to see us, their problem was simple: judgment. As working professionals with kids, their lives were a constant exertion of energy. When they weren't working (Carrie as a nurse and Tom as a partner in an accounting firm), they carted their three children around to sports, dance, and birthday parties. Even though they were busy, they made sure to spend time together every week. Friday was date night, and they always hired a sitter so they could be alone and focus on each other.

The problem, however, was that at home, neither one of them could meet the other's expectations. They gave us an example that was common in their daily life together. Tom cooked and Carrie did the dishes. On one typical evening, he decided to not only cook but do the dishes too as a way of doing something nice for Carrie. As he rinsed the utensils and started to place them in the dishwasher, her smile at his generosity turned to a skeptical frown. She said he hadn't washed them enough. He said that he had. They began to fight and spent the night sleeping in separate bedrooms.

Stress reduction is the goal of learning to manage your alarm; a high level of awareness is key to making that goal attainable. Tom and Carrie were not stressed by the way Tom did the dishes. They were stressed because of their lives. But because they didn't measure their stress levels on a regular basis, they didn't realize it. Because they weren't aware that their stress levels were at a four, five, or six on a regular basis, little tendencies in each other's behavior raised their already heightened stress chemicals into full-scale meltdowns.

After we taught them to measure their stress levels, they came back for a final session and reported the difference. They were still both particular people who liked to do things their own way, and they recounted a recent repeat of the dishwasher incident. Carrie had the same reaction to Tom's way of doing the dishes. Instead of getting angry, he smiled as he noticed his alarm go up, and said, "Focus on the nice thing I'm doing and I promise if they come out dirty, I'll wash them again."

They slept in the same room that night.

## The Personal Control Thermometer

Personal control derives from being able to think clearly so that you have the confidence of knowing you can handle whatever happens in this moment and whatever comes your way. Not perfectly. Not without effort. Not without ups and downs. We want to handle stress well enough to feel hopeful, to be able to step back and realize that our lives have purpose and can be fulfilling even when we feel stressed.

Why then doesn't every stress management class and book tell you to pay attention to your personal control level as well as your stress level? Because when you look at stress mainly as a problem, instead of as a breakdown in the relationship between your thinking and alarm centers, the solution to stress is to stop feeling it. Now that you know about the key role that the thinking center in the brain plays in stress, and the partnership between the thinking center and alarm that is necessary for an optimal brain, you can't miss the importance of checking up regularly on your level of personal control.

Personal control is your confidence that at this moment you can think clearly enough to make good choices and handle the challenges you face. How well your thinking center does in partnering with—not trying to ignore, or get rid of, or turn off—your brain's alarm determines your ability to consistently use stress as a valuable resource like Grete Waitz, the Dalai Lama, or Tom did when he didn't get angry over something as minor as dishes.

Right now, on a scale of one to ten, with one being the lowest and ten being the highest you've ever experienced, rate your level of personal control. Remember, even personal control, as great as it sounds, really is neither good nor bad. It is simply your thinking center sending chemicals through your brain so that you can pay attention and learn. It is your brain and body telling you how you're doing in your life right at this moment.

If your personal control level is very high, an eight or more, that's good to know. It doesn't mean that you're a genius or better than anyone else. It just means that you can tell that you're thinking clearly and calmly. Clear thinking is what gives any of us the deep and dependable feeling of confidence that is the best antidote for stress.

If your personal control level is lower, that is not a problem—it's an invitation to read on and learn about the many ways to activate the thinking center and gain personal control. Do an SOS right now. When the learning brain activates, your level of personal control rises. You already have more personal control than you realize, but most of us don't recognize the intuitive ways in which we use our thinking centers. The problem with not noticing is that we lose the benefit of our own wisdom.

## The Necessity of Reflection

If we don't reflect, we react. The power of our brain is that it can think in numerous and complex ways: imagining, creating, suspecting, incorporating, believing, and adapting. Studies of the brain continue to unlock the myriad ways our brains function to unpack our experiences and understand our relationship to the world around us. What we know for sure, however, is that if we do not reflect, we don't learn.

The importance of checking our stress and personal control levels is that our past experiences and how we remember them will change the way we live in the future. If we don't stop and notice the true depth of what's happening to us—what it feels like and means—we cannot choose the way we will behave. Instead, we become slaves to our alarms, doing what will keep us safe rather than intentionally regulating our thoughts, emotions, and actions.

John Dewey was a pioneer in the field of education who taught that our environments affect our behavior. A philosopher and educational theorist, he was also one of the leading figures in the "new psychology" movement of the late nineteenth century. He was one of the visionaries who realized that humans are more an adaptable organism than a predictable machine. In his book *How We Think*, he uses dozens of descriptors to define and clarify what it is to reflect. None is more valuable than a simple case study he presents in the opening pages.

He tells the story of a man who comes to a crossroad. He's not from the area and he doesn't know where he's going. We know, of course, that at this moment, his alarm flares. He has to decide what to do. He climbs a tree to figure out where he is. He has to look for a sign or something that will pique his memory. Dewey calls this a "forked-road" moment. He writes,

> *As long as our activity glides smoothly along from one thing to another, or as long as we permit our imagination to entertain fancies at pleasure, there is no call for reflection.*

Stated simply, we don't think we need to reflect or measure when our brains function optimally. That all changes, however, when we're stressed because our brains realize something is wrong. He then offers the most important statement about why SOS matters to every human mind.

> *Demand for the solution [of a problem] is the steadying and guiding factor in the entire process of reflection.*

We can't live in alarm world happily. Our alarms demand a solution to any fork in the road. But we can't find the solution unless we pause and think about our circumstances, what they mean, and the options we have.

If your alarm fills your body with too much adrenaline, you can't think. You can't deal with simple choices—like what to eat for dinner that will be healthy and delicious—or the larger challenges—like how you want to live your life. If your alarm sounds too often and too loud, you can't focus on what matters. The alarm is the bell rung in the brain to tell us that we need to reflect. SOS is the first step in opening the learning brain to the process of reflection.

But SOS is not just a crisis intervention or de-escalation technique, although it can be used for that purpose. We don't want you to wait to use it until you're in crisis. To be of the greatest value, SOS is a life skill first, and a call for help only when you need it. In fact, we strongly recommend that you don't use SOS in a crisis or even in a moment of non-critical high stress *until you've practiced and applied it extensively in low-or-no-stress moments.*

Why? The answer is the same as for any life skill. We learn how to drive in a quiet neighborhood before we go on the highway at seventy miles per hour. SOS is no different.

Think of SOS as a mental vitamin. Regular daily doses are the best way to get the fullest benefit. SOS sharpens the mind and increases your awareness of—and therefore your ability to do healthy things for—your body. Being able to think clearly about what's most important in your life is more valuable on a day-to-day basis than in the occasional emergency because it prevents not only many crises but also the worst possible danger other than death: missing the opportunities to create a life full of happiness and meaning.

Yet sometimes we get so stressed, we just can't focus by doing an SOS. That's when we need to recognize our triggers.

# Chapter Eight

# When You Can't SOS: Recognize Triggers

We're about to teach you a way of focusing when everything is falling apart. Don't forget, however: the best way to prevent meltdowns is to practice SOS. Practice often. There's no better time to focus your mind than either when starting something new or when finishing a project or a part of your day. It's a tune-up that prepares you to make the most of whatever you're experiencing, and it makes sure you're paying attention to what's happening in your brain.

So as we begin this new chapter, let's do an SOS to practice what you've learned so far in this section.

Start by *stepping back*. When you're unfocused, your mind is a mental traffic jam of competing thoughts and feelings. Enjoy a moment where all you have to do is free yourself from the clutter.

If you feel tense or fatigued, remember, these are signals from your brain's alarm that your body is out of balance. Stepping back activates your thinking center so it notices your alarm and can begin to turn down the feelings of tension or fatigue in your body.

Now *orient* yourself. Having activated your thinking center, you're ready to fully focus your mind on **one** thing. That **you choose**. Because it is the **most important thing for you** in your whole life right at this moment. Something or someone that is **what you care about and value** more than anything else in your entire life right now.

Each time you orient to what is most important to you, you've recharged and optimized your brain's thinking center. You've put your deepest values and beliefs front and center to guide your mind and your actions. You have just regained control in your life, the ability to think clearly, because you've oriented to what gives you purpose.

Everything changes when you take a few seconds, at most a minute or two, to step back and to orient yourself. Only two minutes, and you've taken back control from your alarm.

Finally, *self-check*. On a scale of one to ten, one being the lowest and ten being the highest you've ever experienced, how much stress are you feeling right now? On a second scale of one to ten, one being the least and ten being the most personal control you've ever felt in your life, how much personal control do you have at this moment?

If you're more than five on stress or less than five in personal control, consider doing another SOS. Not because you've done it wrong or aren't handling stress well enough. It takes intentional practice to translate the science of the brain into feeling grounded and thinking clearly. Doing another SOS is not a sign of failure or that you're a slow learner; it's a sign of dedication and a desire to be healthy. The only failure is the common mistake we all seem to make—letting our minds remain unfocused.

Now that you're focused, you're ready to learn what to do when you're not. Some days the whole world seems to explode. Everywhere we look, there's something else that raises our alarm. These things that stress us out are triggers, and just as stress can be valuable because it is a sign that our life is out of balance, we can use triggers to start thinking clearly again. The second skill in the FREEDOM model is recognizing triggers.

## What Is a Trigger?

The term *trigger* commonly refers to anything unpleasant: an angry comment from a friend or stranger, a traffic jam, a work deadline, or a reminder of the death of someone we cared about. When discovering how your learning brain can notice and turn down your alarm, the definition of a trigger is more specific.

*A trigger is something that causes us to react quickly and negatively without thinking.* When something triggers our alarm—a sound, a word or phrase, another person—it triggers our body to flood with the chemicals that create feelings like anger, fear, guilt, or hopelessness.

The problem is not the trigger itself, however. The feelings we experience are valuable information about whether what we're experiencing is important to us or not. Even difficult, painful experiences can be entirely worth living—like running a marathon or staying up all night to soothe a child. Difficult experiences don't have to trigger us even if they raise the level of stress in our body. The problem is that we don't differentiate what's really triggering us from other parts of an experience that are unpleasant.

For example, consider an angry comment from a friend. It contains triggers such as the exact words that are used, the tone of voice, the facial expression and body language, the place where it occurs, the other people who are there, and its future consequences for you and your relationship to your friend. Each of these elements in the experience is unpleasant. Trying to figure out how to deal with a cluster of triggers big and small can be like trying to get the honey out of a beehive. If you don't know what you're doing, you will get stung.

On the other hand, if you know exactly what to focus on, like a skilled beekeeper, you can be surrounded by triggers and not get stressed. A beekeeper does not try to deal with every single bee. He leaves most of them alone, and they leave the beekeeper alone as well. The beekeeper focuses on the queen bee. When she's not riled, neither are her drones.

When we connect our learning brains and our alarms in the long loop, the learning brain immediately recognizes any triggers that need to be dealt with. When the thinking center attempts to recognize a trigger, like a beekeeper looking for the queen, a fascinating thing happens in our brains: we can begin to shift focus away from feeling stressed (the alarm's call for help) to thinking about whatever is most important to feel, reflect on, or experience.

In every stressful event or situation, there is a swarm of potential triggers. The skill is to find the specific trigger that really matters. The alarm fires no matter how big or small the trigger. Once you've noticed your alarm is firing, your thinking center, as it focuses on figuring out the underlying stress trigger, can turn the alarm down.

This capacity of our brains to focus even when we're a total mess is so important. When we get triggered and don't know why, we can often find ourselves behaving in ways we don't intend. When reacting to a trigger, it's not uncommon for people to

- complain
- yell
- hit
- run away
- withdraw

Triggers usually set off strong alarm reactions before we really know what happened.

Can you think of a time when you felt flooded with feelings and you didn't know why? Or maybe you thought you knew exactly why, but you felt helpless to control your reaction. It's not the trigger that causes the reaction; it's your alarm.

In these moments it can be very difficult to focus by doing an SOS. You can, however, turn on the learning brain and activate your brain's optimal functioning by trying to figure out what's triggering you. Other than absolute life-and-death triggers—like seeing someone with a gun or witnessing a lion in the act of attacking, the reactions we have to triggers are not entirely automatic. Triggers, when unmanaged, can lead to deeply ingrained habitual reactions or compulsions such as addictions or serious anger management problems. But research has proven that even addictive habits, explosive anger, or loss of control due to traumatic or persistent stress can be fundamentally changed *if* you begin by recognizing triggers using the thinking center.

# Hit the Deck

Detective Rodriguez had worked his way up to detective starting with a regular patrol. He rose quickly in the department because there was no one he couldn't make comfortable with his quick wit and easy demeanor. But after Detective Rodriguez was shot on the job, he retired from the police force. It's not that he couldn't still work a desk, but he couldn't handle being around other officers on a daily basis when his leg injury prevented him from being in the field. He began selling cars.

His comfortable style and humor made him an immediate success with customers. That changed, however, during a blowout sale at his dealership. A child accidentally popped a balloon, which then popped four more in one of the gigantic bunches they'd put together for the event. Without knowing why, Detective Rodriguez hit the deck. He was in the middle of finishing a sale with a young couple, and when he realized what he had done, he walked out of the dealership and went home.

When he came in for treatment, he was missing work and afraid to go out at night. He was terrified he was going to overreact again. Even though he knew that he was safe, he felt afraid all the time. Then, as he learned about his brain, how to do SOS, and to recognize that loud sounds triggered him, his confidence came back. He realized he wasn't having the extreme stress response because something was wrong with him, but because his alarm wanted him to never get shot again.

He realized his overreaction had actually been evidence about how powerful his brain truly was. The trigger and his alarm reaction were a reminder to him of how important it is to be safe and have a full life. "It's a total 180 degree change for me," he said, "because I thought I couldn't handle any loud sound. Now I know my brain's taking care of me and even if I overreact again, I can explain to people what's happening."

He went back to work. He started dating, something he hadn't done since his accident, and quickly found a girlfriend. He started telling jokes again.

In his final session, he talked about a birthday party for his girlfriend's daughter. When he walked into the house, his heart almost stopped as he saw a huge bouquet of balloons, every color of the rainbow. But he immediately recognized the trigger. At different parts of the party, he did an SOS, orienting on enjoying his new girlfriend, to remind himself that there was nothing in the room he couldn't handle. Then, as the kids were eating cake, he sat down on the couch to check the score of the football game. Just as he turned on the TV, a little boy popped a balloon right behind him. At that moment, his body flooded with the desire jump off the couch.

But he didn't.

Instead he stood up, walked to the little boy who was about to cry because his balloon popped, carried him to the bouquet, and had him pick out a new one.

## To Recognize Is to Rethink

*Recognizing triggers* is the act of preparing your brain to use the alarm reactions that cause stress as valuable information to move toward living a life that's most meaningful to you.

Can you remember a time when you felt out of control and reacted poorly? What about experiencing other people who had meltdowns because something triggered them? Many things can trigger an alarm reaction. Almost all of us are triggered when someone yells at us, or we feel like we're trapped in a situation without any choices. The power of your learning brain and triggers is twofold: each of us can recognize our triggers in advance before they take control of us, and the moment we attempt to recognize our triggers, we engage the learning brain and begin to focus.

To recognize is to rethink. The act of thinking again from a new perspective rather than getting caught in the rut of reactive alarm thoughts ignites the power of your thinking center and begins to turn down the stress reactions. Triggers are a signal to your alarm that something is wrong:

- Something needs fixing.
- Something should be happening, but isn't.
- Something could be done better.
- Something is not the way you want it to be.

Triggers don't necessarily mean that something terrible is happening. Most often, they are simply situations that need some attention. A trigger that goes unaddressed for years can become more than just a bee buzzing around your head, but a trigger we recognize proves to our alarm that we're in control.

For example, your best friend is a pleaser. She can't say no to anyone, ever. Most of the time, it's not a problem. The problem is that she gets stressed because she's always saying yes to things she really doesn't care about or doesn't want to do. Then she complains to you. The next time you hear her saying yes in what seems to be an attempt to avoid conflict or make someone else like her, that could trigger your alarm to have a major stress reaction. You might feel so angry that you think you want to scream at her or end your relationship, even though nothing appears to have changed from a day, or week, or year ago.

Most stress triggers are like that. They tend to start as mildly unpleasant actions or uncomfortable situations involving other people. Sometimes they are barely tolerable right from the start, but you try to make allowances and see the good in the person or situation in spite of the triggers. Either way, they become intolerable over time. If you wait until that point of no return to recognize the trigger, your alarm reaction often will be so strong that you feel unable to think clearly and control your actions.

It doesn't have to be like that. Recognizing triggers means paying attention to what's not right or what could be better in yourself, your life, and your relationships. The purpose is not to create a "laundry list" of complaints or a private list of grievances that fester and lead to stress reactions. That is what the alarm does; it keeps an endless list of what can go or has gone wrong.

Triggers, and the alarm reactions that they set in motion, are a call to think rather than to react. If you find yourself so frustrated with a friend or family member that you just can't SOS, you can start to think about what is triggering you. It's much easier to think of triggers as annoyances or a justification for either going off on, or shutting down and avoiding, other people. But that's what the alarm will do if the thinking center doesn't get into the act.

Over time, when you reflect about what triggers you, your memory center will remind you of the things that can create stress reactions. Thinking clearly about the triggers before they become a meltdown makes it possible for us to take responsibility for what the trigger is really calling us to do: not react without thinking, but focus on what's most important.

## The MTV Meltdown

When country-pop artist Taylor Swift walked up on stage at the MTV video music awards in 2009, she wore a long, silver sequined gown, her blond hair pinned up. Her second album had earned her four Grammys, including album of the year and a nod for Billboard's artist of the year.

When she said, "Thank you so much" to the MTV crowd, the teenager looked authentically surprised and completely grateful. "I always dreamed what it would be like to maybe win one of these some day, but I never actually thought it would happen. I sing country music so thank you so much for giving me a chance to win a VMA award."

As she got ready to start her next sentence, the cameras showed a close-up of another artist in the applauding audience. When the camera panned back to the stage, Kanye West, a rapper and producer who had won fourteen Grammys himself, held the microphone. At first, Swift didn't know what was happening. Then West said, "Taylor, I'm going to let you finish, but Beyoncé had one of the best videos of all time." The crowd was shocked. He repeated, "One of the best videos of all time," handed Swift the microphone, and left the stage. One of music's most successful artists had just been triggered into a full-scale alarm meltdown in front of the entire world.

On *The Ellen DeGeneres Show*, West admitted he had been working too hard for too long without a break and that his mother had died. Think of how high his baseline stress level would have been. In explaining that night he said, "For your entire world to crash off of a moment of sincerity or alcohol, or whatever it is, to lose…" He started to laugh and Ellen interrupted and said, "Usually the alcohol rules out the sincerity part."

But in the candid interview he said, "In some ways I feel like I'm a soldier of culture." He felt he had to speak out about things that "constantly get denied for years and years and years…I can't lie about it any more to sell records."

At the awards, he was exhausted. He'd been drinking. *He lost his mom.* Taylor Swift winning triggered Kanye West's alarm. His alarm was already on high alert, and in that moment he perceived the white woman winning over the black woman as an issue of race. Right or wrong, his jumping up on stage occurred because of the trigger. If he had intentionally recognized his triggers, he still would have been triggered by Beyoncé losing, but he would have been able to think clearly about how to react to the situation. In the moment, he would have been in control.

Following the media uproar at his reaction, he literally did an extended SOS. He stepped back from his life as a celebrity and went to Japan. Then he oriented to his music in Hawaii for six months. When he had checked himself, he was willing to talk to Ellen and surprised everyone by saying what really happened that night.

What happened to West happens to most of us every day. We're tired. We're flooded with adrenaline from the needs of work or the kids. We're overwhelmed by thoughts of bills to pay and too much to do. Then someone cuts us off in traffic and we start screaming.

West said to Ellen about his time away, "It was time to take a break, to develop more as a person, as a creative, and to focus more on my thoughts and my ideas, and what I wanted to bring to the world."

After the fact, West recognized his trigger so clearly he could describe it on national TV in an authentic way, and he was able to talk about his values and what mattered to him. If we can recognize our triggers and find the same clarity before we melt down, we can prevent ourselves from acting in a way that causes us to lose control.

Since that incident, West has only performed on stage at award shows.

## What Triggers Do to the Brain

Brain studies with people who have been through major traumatic stressors such as war or abuse have given us an increasingly clear picture of what happens when triggers occur. Thinking about terrifying or horrifying past experiences tends to activate the brain's alarm powerfully for these individuals, especially if they're having intense stress reactions in their day-to-day-lives. While we don't know exactly what's happening in their brains in daily life—because the technology to scan brains on a 24/7 basis hasn't been available both for technical and ethical reasons—we do know that when people replay an extremely distressing memory as if they were witnessing the events again for the first time, images of their brains show that the amygdala becomes highly activated.

At the same time, the memory and thinking centers in their brains, which ordinarily work just fine, tend to be poorly activated. This is the opposite of what happens when people who don't suffer from PTSD replay stressful memories from their lives. Those individuals' amygdalas do get revved up, but not nearly as much, and the prefrontal cortex (thinking center) and hippocampus (memory center) tend to be quite strongly activated as well.

Evidence from brain imaging studies of people who are seriously depressed or anxious shows a similar pattern of intense alarm reactivity and underperforming thinking and memory centers when those individuals are confronted by stressful laboratory situations. We don't know if this pattern of brain activity is exactly what happens when people who haven't had their alarms amped up by trauma get stressed in daily life, but it is likely to be the case.

What we can say for now is that brain science strongly suggests that triggers result in a strong reaction from the brain's alarm. If the thinking and memory centers are equally activated, the alarm reaction does not appear to escalate out of control, and the trigger actually sets in motion a process of thoughtful reflection that can lead to good choices and reduced rather than increased stress. It's only when the thinking and memory centers are *not* fully activated that stress reactions lead to reactive choices and chronic stress.

## How to Recognize Triggers

Every time Debbie's husband told her he had to go away for a business trip, she told us, she became rageful. She felt like she wanted to put him in a closet, lock the door, and walk away.

A flood of feelings like this comes from what our alarm sees that our conscious brain does not. Debbie's alarm knew that when her spouse was gone, she was lonely. She had to work full-time. She had to take care of the kids and the house all on her own.

Our alarm pulls out memories from our memory center when what's happening in the present reminds us of past difficult or traumatic experiences. For Debbie, this happened when something in the present triggered her memory of how upset she'd felt as a child when her father traveled on business. Hearing "I have to go away" was all it took to bring her back to being three and watching her dad walk down the driveway. She wondered if he would ever come home. Her spouse leaving triggered the memory, and she found herself reliving the fear that her father wouldn't come home as if it was happening all over again.

Is this normal? Absolutely. The brain's alarm doesn't grow up; it retains a child's perspective no matter how old or mature we become. The alarm also doesn't distinguish past, present, and future. If something was a problem in the past or could be a problem in the future, as far as the alarm is concerned it *is* a problem *right now*.

Let's go through a list of the things than can trigger people and do a simple exercise to make sure the power of recognizing triggers is clear. We can be triggered by

- specific things people do
- specific things people say
- places
- activities
- times of day, dates, seasons, or anniversaries
- bodily feelings like fatigue, pain, or gut reactions

Which one of these categories immediately strikes you as a way in which you're triggered?

Now pick a specific example: a time when you were angry, a person you don't spend time with any more, a place you avoid.

Hold that example in your mind for a second.

Can you feel the adrenaline? When we're triggered we can literally feel our alarm get us ready to protect ourselves.

There is nothing wrong with being triggered; what's usually missed is that *the trigger itself is essential to managing stress reactions.* Most people, when they feel they've been triggered, want to know what to do. That desire for instant relief is possible, but it is not found by *doing* anything to react to the trigger.

Instead, the relief and calm come when we're able to think clearly about what's happening: what is the trigger, how does it make sense that this would set off our alarm, and what do we need to think about so we're in control? Clear thinking is what we need to *do* in order to handle a trigger that's set off an alarm reaction.

Within a trigger is the substance of what your alarm finds dangerous. The skill of recognizing triggers is that, by stepping back to identify what the trigger is, you will engage your thinking center and begin to turn down the alarm. Or, you can begin to notice triggers earlier, so that your alarm isn't blindsided.

If Debbie knew that people leaving her was a trigger, it's not that she'd suddenly be very happy when her husband went away. But she would be able to say something like, "Tell me about the trip." If it was clear that he had to go, they could make a plan to stay in contact so that she would know that he was safe. If he didn't have to go, she could then negotiate for him to stay home. Either way, she needs a sense of control she didn't have as a child.

Too many of us overreact, and when triggered, we don't talk to people we love for the next three days. You'd be surprised how normal that kind of overreaction is in relationships.

To regain control we can recognize very specific triggers. Taylor Swift was not Kanye West's trigger; it was his perception of continued racism in the music business symbolized by a white woman receiving an award over a black woman. Your triggers are usually attached to personal values or goals, and the trigger is your brain perceiving that something or someone is stopping you from experiencing what's important to you.

We need to learn to recognize triggers because the alarm doesn't want you to be angry or do something foolish or harmful. It's actually trying to help you avoid feeling that way or doing crazy things. But it's not good at developing creative solutions. It only knows how to point out what's wrong and to pull the first memories it can find from the memory center for ways to solve the problem.

If your alarm fixates on a certain solution, like not speaking to a spouse if he goes on a business trip because that's what you did when you were a child and you missed your father, that's actually an alarm reaction. What matters is that you first recognize your spouse's leaving as a trigger—a trigger that's led your alarm to activate the memory of feeling abandoned by your father. Then in the future you won't immediately go to the first option that your alarm can find in your memory center.

We want to fill our daily memory centers with clear thoughts about both what's most important to us and what gets in the way of what we care about. When we recognize our power to identify triggers, and our memory centers know what triggers us, we can think more clearly about what we really want to experience in any given moment.

## Can Someone Else Turn on My Alarm?

Before we move on to the most powerful ways you can orient, we have a final important point about triggers: one of the most common sources of secondhand stress is other people. Spouses, children, parents, friends, coworkers, strangers, and that person at the gym who always talks to you and won't just let you work out: not only can they turn on your alarm, they will, almost every day. In the modern world, it's like we're all traumatized by how much contact we have with other people and the way they treat us.

Often, we're triggered because their alarm has been triggered. It's like a child who wants ice cream and won't stop screaming when a parent says no. The screaming child will trigger a parent until she figures out what triggers her about her child's alarm reactions.

Once you've consistently paid attention to what triggers you, the difference is that you can handle what the alarm does to your mind and body. You become aware that when others have a stress reaction or meltdown, it's the result of not using their brains' thinking centers to help their alarm regain confidence and security. And you don't have to make that same mistake.

For instance, you go to a meeting with a colleague you truly enjoy working with. Most times, when she is on your schedule, just the thought of spending time with her makes your day better. But this time, when you get together, she is different. She is more defensive. Her behavior isn't directed at you, but you notice she's not her usual self. This same sort of nagging feeling that something isn't right happens with family, friends, and even with strangers. Our alarms can tell when a situation isn't optimal.

You were already tired that day, and your colleague's defensiveness triggers you. If you didn't recognize your alarm firing, instead of going for a walk when you get home, you pour a drink. Instead of asking your spouse how her day was, you ignore everyone. You react instead of choosing the life you want to experience, and now you alarm everyone around you.

When you intentionally recognize your triggers, however, you let your alarm remain on until you determine what caused it to send its messages (the stress reactions). It might be after the meeting or even in the middle of it if you're really attentive to your alarm, but you won't try to deny it or drown it; you'll sit with it.

Instead of listening to the news on the car ride home, you'll let your learning brain process the experience, trusting that you can figure out what triggered you. You go for a walk with your spouse instead of pouring a drink. You'll talk about why the experience made you feel stressed. If you need to, you'll even be comfortable waiting a few days to let your mind fully process the experience, so you can wisely choose how to next approach your colleague with your concerns about her behavior.

When you know your optimal brain can help you understand your triggers, even if your alarm goes off again, it won't be something to fear or dread. When our brains are clear about what's most important to us, we know exactly what to focus on after we recognize our triggers. That's the topic of the next section: filling our memory center with the most powerful ways for you to orient and reduce stress.

# Part III

## Three Ways to Orient before Stress Takes Over

# Chapter Nine

# Empower Your Emotions

As you become more and more comfortable with focusing your thinking center, you can literally take control over what's happening in your brain and body. The next three skills in the FREEDOM model aren't new skills; rather, they are a deeper application of SOS. These are the three forms of thinking Julian's research has identified as the most powerful ways to orient. You can literally choose the emotions and thoughts that guide you when you focus your mind on what is most important to you rather than reacting to where you are and what's happening to you.

To deepen our ability to focus, the first place we'll practice using SOS is with our emotions. We can't say for sure which comes first, the feeling or the thought, but most of us are familiar with the emotions that come with stress before we recognize the thoughts that stress us. For instance, when you're angry at someone you care about, someone you like and want to spend time with, in the moment of anger, you can't feel love. The danger for most of us is that we take these moments of anger, embarrassment, or anxiety, and we let them control how we live. In our relationships, we put walls up or we leave people over negative emotional experiences.

Instead, we have the power, if we choose, to switch our focus and orient to what we want to feel about that person. We can replace anger with memories of feeling pleasure or warmth. We're about to show you how to choose the way you want to feel and how to fill the files of your memory center with emotions you want to remember. To continue recognizing the personal control you have, we'll look next at the first "E" in FREEDOM: *empower your emotions.*

## What Is Emotion?

Every stress reaction triggered by your brain's alarm brings with it a bundle of emotions. Emotions are the first things that we notice after our bodies send us a message that we're having a stress reaction. The body's physical feelings that signal a stress reaction, like tensing up, sweating, and that raw pit in your stomach, are the early warning signs.

*Emotions are the thinking center's instant summary of bodily reactions.* Although most of us think that emotions arise mysteriously somewhere between the body and mind, they aren't that complicated. An emotion is the thinking center's translation of bodily feelings into thoughts. For example, when you feel scared, it's because there is danger lurking. The thinking center uses that feeling as information to try to figure out what's going on and what to do about it.

After looking out into the environment for triggers, the next thing the thinking center does is create a mental "headline" to explain why the alarm has fired up physical stress reactions. Remember, the alarm often causes the reaction before we're even aware of it. It's always looking out for you. The following list describes an emotion, what the alarm perceives, and the action it wants you to take to stay safe.

- Fear: you may be in danger; be on guard.
- Anxiety: something may go wrong; check for potential problems.
- Sadness: someone or something important to you is gone (or may go away); find new happiness.
- Guilt: you did something wrong; figure it out and fix it.
- Embarrassment: you're not measuring up to your (or someone else's) standards; work harder or smarter.
- Shame: you're violating your basic beliefs or values; be true to yourself.

- Anger: something or someone is harming you or others you care about; protect yourself or them.
- Disgust: something smells bad, literally or figuratively; get rid of it.
- Horror: something too terrible to be believed is happening; get away!
- Terror: something too terrible to survive is happening; run!
- Boredom: nothing interesting is happening; find something you care about to do.
- Frustration: something that should be fixable isn't getting fixed; find a new way.
- Annoyance: something that should be minor is becoming a big problem; find another new way.
- Insecurity: no one is looking out for you; remember your optimal brain is always there to help you find the life that matters to you.

What do you do with messages like these? Generally, we try to ignore them. We try to talk ourselves out of feeling the way we do. We just want the feeling to stop. These common reactions are exactly that: reactions. They are following the short loop and living according to the messages of your emotional brain.

If you pay attention to what your emotions tell you and give careful thought to how those messages can help you handle challenges and stressors, however, you can take charge of your life instead of letting your emotions run it. Empowering your emotions means you choose what you want to feel.

But how can anyone remember to think about the message from our emotions when we're ready to erupt with anger or so depressed we don't want to move? Empowering your emotions means using your thinking center to learn what your body is telling you.

## Empowered While Powerless

What can make a person feel more powerless than to be held prisoner in her own home?

Aung San Suu Kyi's is the first of three stories we want to tell about paying attention to and focusing on emotion to turn down the stress response and think clearly. Known as "The Lady" to virtually everyone in her country of Myanmar (Burma), she was a rising and charismatic politician when she was placed under house arrest. The daughter of a freedom fighter father and a mother who served as a diplomat, she was educated at Oxford. She married and raised her two children in Britain before returning to the capital city of Rangoon in 1988 to tend to her sick mother.

When she arrived, Myanmar was in upheaval. Students and office workers revolted against the dictatorship. She took up the cause leading peace rallies and non-violent protest. She said, "I could not, as my father's daughter, remain indifferent to all that was going on."

A military coup ended the uprising, and when the government called elections in 1990, the National League for Democracy party she helped form and lead as general secretary won the majority of the parliamentary seats. The junta refused to recognize the results, which might have even made her prime minister, and she remained under house arrest. Fearing that she was a threat to the peace of the country, the government held her under house arrest for fifteen of the next twenty-one years.

How did she deal with the fear? She woke up each day, never knowing if she—like many others in her country—would be thrown into prison and never heard from again, or executed. By all accounts, she lived a very simple and austere existence with very little human contact. At her house by a lake, her life seemed to pass her by—but not really.

In a speech in 1990, titled "Freedom from Fear," she said, "Fearlessness may be a gift but perhaps more precious is the courage acquired through endeavor, courage that comes from cultivating the habit of refusing to let fear dictate one's actions, courage that could be described as 'grace under pressure'—grace which is renewed repeatedly in the face of harsh, unremitting pressure."

Her speech tells the story at the very beginning of her journey. She focused on "courage." Courage is a feeling. It's an emotion we can experience and recall from our memory center. As her father had fought for freedom, as her heroes like Gandhi and Martin Luther King Jr. had struggled nonviolently until they achieved freedom for their people, she returned again and again to the feeling of courage.

In a situation like Suu Kyi's, inevitably feelings of intense anger would come: anger at the injustice, anger at being away from her husband who ultimately died of cancer, anger at the world for not doing something for her and her people. Yet she did not let her alarm feelings get in the way of her optimal feelings. In the occasional photographs of her over the years, was a face that expressed an unbreakable determination combined with implacable calm. Her face aged over time, but her composure never seemed to falter.

What could she have been thinking to achieve such a serene and powerful focus? How did she live with, let alone empower, an emotion like anger?

She empowered her emotions by transforming the inevitable alarm reactions into calm perseverance. She may have struggled with impulses from her alarm to retaliate with aggression or to resign herself to failure, but what we saw was the ultimate achievement: she created a partnership between her alarm and her thinking center. She honored the desire of her alarm for safety while also honoring her quest for freedom. In the latest elections, she has become a member of the Burmese Parliament.

But you don't have to be world-famous or a Nobel Prize winner like Aung San Suu Kyi to empower your emotions so you don't feel trapped. We take care of two very different kinds of women in our work: mothers in poverty and suburban moms. In totally different economic conditions, they suffer from the same challenge that Suu Kyi had to overcome: isolation.

Joann is twenty-nine, a single mom with three kids and two jobs. She struggles each month to pay the rent on her two-bedroom apartment. Keri is thirty-five. She has two children and left her executive position at a financial services firm to raise her family.

Joann is either caring for her children or working as a nurse's aide and for a cleaning service. She never gets time to herself or a chance to focus on anything she wants to do. The only time she's not caring for others is at church, where the older women watch her children while she sings in the choir.

Keri's husband is also a successful executive, but he travels and is rarely home during the week. They live in a five-bedroom house, but she doesn't know her neighbors. To get even a moment to herself, she has to call a babysitter. She can't shower or go to the bathroom without being interrupted. She never has time with adults, except when she goes to work out and leaves her kids with the child-care service at her health club.

Both of their stories are common, and when they came to see us, they reported the same feelings of frustration and loneliness. They didn't want to feel angry at their children, but both were starting to yell at their kids. They each felt like their children had stolen their lives.

After teaching Joann and Keri SOS, we asked them to think about a moment when they felt connected to their children. Joann talked about her oldest child at a spelling bee. Keri told us she feels at home with her kids before bed when she reads them stories. In both cases, when we asked them to self-check their stress and level of personal control after recalling feelings of connection, they felt at ease and found that they could think clearly about how important their children were.

As they continued to practice SOS, focusing on the emotions they wanted to feel about their lives and children as well as paying attention to the emotions their alarms evoked, their life situations didn't miraculously change. Joann still had financial concerns and Keri still struggled with solo parenting. But both discovered—and this is common with our studies of servicemen and servicewomen returning from combat, prisoners in the justice system, and adults and children who are simply tired from busy lives—the ability to choose what to do next when they felt overwhelmed.

So what happened to Suu Kyi and these two moms? What made it possible for their different situations to have a similar emotional flavor? They used negative emotions as a reminder to purposefully recall other emotions that gave their lives a sense of importance. The act of recalling the full range of their emotions, not just the alarm emotions, created new memories of how rich their emotional life was. Then they had a choice about which emotion to focus on.

## Emotions and the Brain

Emotions are the colored lights and icons on our mental dashboards. They are a message from the body to pay attention to something, a request or recommendation for us to act. The exact form that the emotion takes is determined by how the alarm relays that message.

*Reactive* emotions are messages from the brain's alarm that something is wrong and needs to be fixed or made safer. As we've discussed, it won't work to attempt to remove the negative emotions and put some positive emotions in their place. A riled-up alarm will send even more negative emotions if it is ignored or shut out. In fact, we want our thinking centers to notice these alarm-driven feelings so that we know to pay attention when there is a problem. The reason they are painful is that there really is something wrong in our current situation and our alarm calls on us to recognize and do something about it. But that doesn't mean that we have to let those reactive emotions control our entire lives.

*Optimal* emotions are what we feel when we focus on what's most impor-tant to us as well as to the reactive message from the alarm. These are the emotions like joy, peace, and satisfaction, which result from the thinking center and alarm working together. But the thinking center can't force the alarm to accept an optimal emotion, without actually dealing with the threat (whether it is real or imagined). If the alarm is activated, it will escalate its distress calls rather than accepting and enjoying the positive feelings.

When the brain is working optimally, however, we remember to first have our thinking center pay attention to the alarm emotions, and then add to these emotions that reflect what we want to experience (feelings based on our deeper values and goals). This combination turns down the alarm and puts the reactive feelings in perspective.

We can think, at our leisure, about what we want to feel. Our daily and blue-moon memories can be mined for the best feelings of our lives. We can both experience optimal feelings in the moment, as we're having an experience that's most important to us, and we can remember the moments when our lives were optimal. Too many people don't take advantage of this ability because we react through life rather than living it.

When you pay attention to emotions, you empower yourself by noticing the parts of life you need to prepare for. This allows you to activate your thinking center and quickly understand what's going on. If you notice emotions when a stress reaction starts (or is about to start), this empowers your thinking center to make a plan for what to do. Emotions don't cause you to overreact. Emotions *prevent* overreactions by the alarm. Emotions are a wake-up call that allows us to recognize that we need to pay attention. If we pay attention to them, they serve a clear purpose: to ensure that a situation that triggers us, and the inevitable alarm feelings, don't overwhelm the optimal emotions we feel most deeply.

## Don't Minimize the Message

When Peter started having panic attacks in the middle of the night, he didn't tell anyone. A successful small-business owner, he hoped it was his tendency to consume quarts of ice cream before bed. Because he worked sixty and sometimes seventy hours a week keeping his appliance store and repair business going, he didn't exercise enough and he ate only when he had time. But the attacks started getting worse.

As he drove down the highway at the end of one long day, an attack came on suddenly. It felt like his chest was going to burst and he could barely get his car to the side of the road. When he came to us, his doctor told him that he needed to change his lifestyle. He had begun working less and working out, but he didn't want to use medication and he was still waking up in the middle of the night.

The same emotions that can clue us in to what's going on and what we need to do to handle a trigger event or situation can become a big problem. When we ignore or shut down our emotions, they can escalate into meltdowns of the fight, flight, or flee variety. But in truth, this is not the fault of our emotions. When emotions seem out of control, it's because *they've been hijacked by the brain's alarm*. Emotions can be used by the alarm to hold us hostage when the alarm is not reassured by the thinking center that a situation or problem is being handled.

In Peter's case, as his business grew, he began to worry that he couldn't sustain the pace. He came from a family that never asked for help, so instead of asking for more from his employees, he did what he should have been delegating to them. As he became more successful and bought a new house and cars, he worried he wouldn't be able to maintain his lifestyle. He'd been anxious for years, but just tried to put the worry out of his head by working harder.

Sound familiar? It's a mistake to take the commonsense approach and try to ignore or minimize the messages sent by our brains' alarms. Remember, that only causes the alarm to up the ante and increase the volume of its demands for attention. Like triggers, emotions can get blown up into major crises or catastrophes by the alarm when we don't take the alarm's caution signals seriously.

On the other hand, when the thinking center responds by showing respect for the emotions generated by the alarm, the alarm turns down the volume of stress chemicals. That's what causes us to feel more peaceful rather than agitated and, ultimately, like we're going to melt down. Peter felt great about his business and the work he did for his customers, even as he worked too hard and worried about the future. When he started to feel the anxiety in his body rise, he learned to recall the feeling of a happy customer. When he couldn't sleep, reminding himself of that feeling helped him turn down his alarm.

The external situation may still be stressful or present problems, but the alarm calms down and cooperates when we use our thinking center to retrieve memories of what we want to feel. The brain's messages are then an opportunity not just to *feel* the emotions delivered, but to understand them using the brain's thinking center. Our thinking centers can figure out what an emotion means. When they do, we can discern what needs to change in our lives to take advantage of the message the emotion makes painfully clear. And in so doing, our clear thinking helps us feel calm and confident again.

## The Pain and Exultation of Creativity

Gustave Flaubert, author of *Madame Bovary* and *Memoirs of a Madman*, once complained bitterly in a letter to a friend, "You don't know what it is to stay a whole day with your head in your hands, trying to squeeze your unfortunate brain so as to find a word."

Writer's block.

It is the bane of a creative mind, and the inevitable reality of an artist unaware of the alarm. Coleridge, Tolstoy, Woolf, Faulkner: men and women, young and old, all of us can experience the paralysis, which makes it impossible to create. It happens to every kind of right-brain creative—painters, designers, actors, and even athletes. None of us, if we do not know how to empower our emotions, can experience the graceful prowess of our optimal brain without the terror and anguish of the alarm blocking our creativity.

Ernest Hemingway drove an ambulance during World War I, ran with the bulls, hunted the wildest beasts in Africa, and when asked what scared him most in the world, he said, "A blank piece of paper." Writer's block or any other block to our thinking is a form of anxiety. It's the self-doubt that we won't be able to do what we did before. To the artist the moment creative thought freezes, the paralysis feels insurmountable. But, in fact, what's happening is the alarm wanting to prevent us from getting hurt: for Hemingway, having written well before, his alarm didn't want him to write poorly in the future.

Hemingway described his process for overcoming writer's block in *A Moveable Feast*.

*Sometimes when I was starting a new story and I could not get it going, I would sit in front of the fire and squeeze the peel of the little oranges into the edge of the flame and watch the sputter of blue that they made. I would stand and look out over the roofs of Paris and think, "Do not worry. You have always written before and you will write now. All you have to do is write one true sentence. Write the truest sentence you know." So finally I would write one true sentence, and then go on from there.*

Notice his first sentence: "Do not worry." That absolutely will turn up most people's anxiety even further. Our alarm is supposed to worry, and in front of a blank page, knowing the purpose is writing, the alarm will only fill your body with more painful emotions. But his other words are the kind of sage advice that allowed him to win the Nobel Prize.

"You've written before." "Write one true sentence." "Write the truest thing you know." He recalled the feeling of writing well; the emotion of what it felt like to capture what he really thought on paper. That's exactly what our alarm needs to allow us to push past the emotional flooding that comes with trying to be creative and struggling to pull it off.

He knew how to stave off writers block as well. In a piece for *Esquire*, he wrote,

*The best way is always to stop when you are going good and when you know what will happen next. If you do that every day…you will never be stuck. Always stop while you are going good and don't think about it or worry about it until you start to write the next day. That way your subconscious will work on it all the time. But if you think about it consciously or worry about it you will kill it and your brain will be tired before you start.*

The reason this advice is so pure is that he is choosing what he wants to focus on feeling. When he felt good and knew what he was going to work on next, he had the feeling of confidence that he could do it again.

The learning brain doesn't forget the feeling that we're ready to keep working the next day because we have something important to write, or paint, or design. That ability to choose what to feel becomes a permanent pattern of emotion when we know why the difficult things we do are worth doing. When you choose to pay attention to emotions that give your life a sense of meaning and value, nothing ultimately can block your power to create.

But what if people don't like what you create? That's just another chance to empower your emotions.

## The Practice of Empowering Emotions

Emotions are neither right nor wrong, but many times we treat them as if they are good or bad. We judge our emotions because they cause us pain or pleasure. Emotions are either instinctual, coming from our alarms, or they are cognitive, coming from our learning brains.

Just because our bodies react to a particular situation based on the alarm doesn't mean we need to continue to feel that way. If you grew up afraid of the dark, believing that monsters lived in the shadows, that doesn't mean as an adult darkness has to spark fear.

To show you how you can empower your emotions, both when you're having a stress reaction and when you simply want to enjoy the rich resources stored in your memory center, let's return to SOS. In every moment, using your thinking center to focus, you can reach into your memory center and find the emotion that is most important for you to experience in this moment.

Let's try it.

Step back. Sweep your mind clear. Notice what you see, hear, and feel in your body, or in the environment around you.

Now that pathways between your alarm and thinking and memory centers are open, you can think clearly. Come with us on a brief tour of your mind.

What was your favorite vacation ever? Or the place where you can truly retreat? It could be at home, or all the way around the world. Who was there that made the place or the experience special? Put the book down for a few moments and play the images and movies stored in your memory center.

As you enjoy the rich memories, notice one more thing. What is the one optimal emotion that you're feeling? What is the emotion that captures all that is good about this experience or place? What emotion sums up the meaning of the place and the people you were with? There is no right or wrong answer, but the emotion to focus on will be one that represents how you feel when you're at your very best.

Here are some examples:

- Serenity
- Joy
- Peace
- Happiness
- Contentment
- Pride
- Love
- Hope
- Fulfillment
- Enthusiasm
- Tranquility
- Comfort
- Interest
- Security

Where is your stress on a scale of one to ten, ten being the highest stress you've ever experienced and one being the least stress and best you've ever felt? Your stress level won't always instantly go down to one or two when you do an SOS, but when you include an optimal emotion in your focusing you will often find that this refreshes your mind. In your body, you will feel a very pleasant drop in your stress level. Your life may still be stressful, but your thinking center is focused. Whether your stress level changes or not, you'll find that your level of personal control will rise as you become aware of optimal emotions.

If you could feel the happiness and peace of sitting in the sun at the beach, or the pleasure of watching your kids play with Mickey and Minnie, or the deep quiet relaxation of fishing with your dad or cooking with your mom (or fishing with your mom and cooking with your dad), you've just had an experience of empowering your emotions. You just chose the feeling on which you wanted to focus your mind. Pause on that for just a second. You just chose what you wanted to feel.

Where is your personal control on a scale of one to ten, ten being the most control you've ever felt in your life and one being totally confused and out of control?

Your feelings do not always have to be reactive. How you feel does not have to be dictated by the triggers that surround you. Or by the fears and worries that preoccupy your brain's alarm. When you notice a negative emotion, you can empower that feeling as a reminder to focus. When you focus on what you want to feel, you empower the memories of past emotions that can turn down your alarm in the present.

Now, if you couldn't do it, there's nothing wrong with you. Imagining your favorite vacation wasn't the right image to introduce you to this version of orienting. Do an SOS focusing on a memory that, at this moment, lets you feel the emotion you want to experience. It doesn't have to be deep or complicated. It could be feeling happy eating your favorite food or sitting next to your favorite person. Or you might imagine the exhilaration of driving with the windows down on a spring day. You can pull the feeling from your memory, and what we know for sure is that every person can learn this skill.

But you have to practice. The alarm wants to run your life until you prove you're thinking clearly. And when your response to an experience that causes stressful emotion is SOS, that emotion is empowered and so are you. Now you're ready to go into a conflict conversation feeling calm, because you did SOS on past conversations that went well. Now you can take on a work challenge like a presentation with everything on the line and pull up feelings of confidence from past successes. When you practice orienting to emotions you want to experience, you can wake up each morning aware that you choose the way you want to feel.

## Before and After

*Someone you love, trust, and care about yells at you.*

How do you feel?

This ten-word vignette may have triggered an alarm reaction about an experience you had recently, or memories of a relationship with a parent, sibling, or loved one where the person hurt you. The memory of the feeling may have come quickly. It may have been linked to a face, name, or experience.

The memory is there to keep you safe.

But it doesn't have to rule what you feel right now. Whatever caused the person to yell at you—whether something you did, intentionally or not, or a random circumstance that caused the other person's alarm to fire and they yelled, the memory is to prevent that experience from happening again.

But the anger or pain you felt when they yelled at you, that's not the only memory you have stored for that person. Before they yelled at you, you cared about the person. Whether that feeling was appreciation like we feel about coworkers and people who help us or a deeper affection like we have for friends and family, our memory center has files we can access in addition to the fear and sadness we feel when remembering the yelling. If it was a boss whom you respected before he or she yelled, when the alarm emotions recede, you return to a place of respect and to feelings that reflect the value that that relationship previously had.

You don't forget that someone yelled at you, but if you recall the emotions of appreciation and respect that led you to value that person in the first place, you *can* choose which feeling you want to focus on. This doesn't erase or cancel out the alarm emotions you're experiencing, it simply gives you the full range of your emotions to work with as you decide how to deal with the person in the future.

Most of us don't choose to return to the optimal emotions we feel about someone because we don't realize we have that power. We let our alarm rule the day. Your emotions are not entirely enigmatic. We should react to people who trigger our alarms. We can also regulate the alarm reaction by recalling the optimal emotion we want as our regular experience when thinking about or spending time with the person who yelled.

Empowering emotion is more complicated, however, when we experience trauma. Trauma is our emotional response to a terrible event. Abuse, war, poverty: the worst traumas leave a permanent memory that can plague people their whole lives.

What's scientifically interesting about trauma is that what traumatizes one person may have no lasting effect on another individual. Seeing a terrible car accident may haunt someone, and the person who was in the wreck may simply be grateful to have survived and rarely think of the event in the future.

People who experience trauma cannot instantly overcome the emotional flooding associated with the trauma. And, even after trauma, research has shown that the feelings we had before, when we felt safe and in control, can be accessed by the thinking center as an emotion. Optimum emotions can be accessed even when the alarm is triggered, if you know to look for them. That's the power of SOS; in this case it allows you to focus on the emotion that's most important for you to feel in this moment.

The key to empowering emotions is remembering that the painful emotion is there to keep you safe. It may not be a happy feeling, but it contains a crucial two-part message: the call to be alert and safe from your alarm, and the offer to reconnect with the feeling of living the life that matters to you. Empowering emotions can give you incredible personal control, if you're paying attention. And it's only the first of three powerful ways to orient.

# Chapter Ten

# Exercise Your Core Values

As we continue to deepen our experience practicing SOS, the second area to work on is values. Everyone knows that some thoughts are more helpful than others. For example, what if you had to choose between thinking "I'm a total failure and my life is a disaster" versus "I'm facing some scary challenges that are pushing me way out of my comfort zone"? It's clear that the second idea, while genuinely capturing the situation, focuses the brain in a fundamentally different way.

That choice, between different ways of expressing the thought in order to decide what we believe is true, is the inspiration for the widely practiced approach to psychotherapy called "cognitive behavior therapy," or CBT. Serious psychological disorders like depression and anxiety can turn a person's mind into a prison of negative thoughts. Tens of thousands of people have benefited from receiving CBT and learning that they have the power to choose what they think.

It's one thing to know the difference between language that is helpful and intrusive thoughts that make stress worse, and another to be able to find and hold on to helpful ideas when you're feeling really stressed. Everything you know from your life experiences, from your role models, or from resources like CBT, can seem worthless at that moment.

But now you know what's really happening when stress reactions seem to trap you in a web of unhelpful judgments. All your skills for thinking effectively are still intact. Everything you've learned about focusing on helpful thoughts when you need to get through upsetting experiences are still true. Your brain's alarm is sending high-stress messages to every part of your body, and your thinking center needs to help the alarm turn itself down.

Instead of dozens of fractured, fragmented, and out-of-control thoughts racing through your mind, you can choose to focus your brain on what you find most calming and helpful. It's not a magical formula or a Jedi-mind trick. Alarm thoughts don't have to be the only soundtrack playing in your mind. Alarm thoughts only take over when the thinking center isn't paying attention to them. You can engage your thinking center to *pay attention to alarm thoughts* instead of trying to ignore or avoid them.

But how? What do you need to think, in order to get your thinking center back on track, when alarm reactions are making it almost impossible to think clearly? The second "E" in FREEDOM is to *exercise your core values.*

## What Is a Core Value?

*A value is your belief in something's worth or importance. A core value is your belief in what's most important to you.* In your life, certain ideas rule your world. You recycle because you want to live green. You exercise because you believe your body is a temple. You sacrifice your personal wants because you value your children's happiness more than your own. Every moment, we make choices based on our values. The problem is most of us don't realize it. We react to our surroundings and live based on the thoughts our alarm and reward centers of the emotional brain instruct us to follow.

We don't recognize we're living our values when we buy a certain food at the grocery store or spend extra time working rather than getting home to be with our families. We don't notice when the alarm sneaks in a thought and we don't focus on what's really important to us. For instance, you're at a community gathering and you see someone you don't recognize. You start toward him to introduce yourself. You value being a good neighbor, and you want to make sure the person feels welcome. Then, as you get closer, you see the person looks like an old friend from college who rejected you. You have an intrusive thought, "This person could hurt me too." You start to feel anxious and pass the person by, instead going to talk to people you already know.

None of us mean to get carried away by our alarm thoughts, but we do. The emotional brain can overwhelm our thinking centers if we don't know what thoughts to focus on. We're designed well, though: the brain's thinking center knows something that the alarm doesn't. Remember, for the alarm, survival is everything. For the thinking center, *learning* is everything. The learning that the thinking center thrives on, the kind of thought it loves to focus on, is the "aha" experience. The "aha" experience is a moment of recognition, whether of something new or something you've always known and rediscover, that becomes a thought that expresses who you are at your core.

When you discover something that is important to you, your thinking center sends a clear and helpful message to your alarm: "This will make life better." Now the pathways in your brain are open. Your core values are the thoughts that turn down your alarm because they express what's interesting enough to actually enhance the quality of your moment-to-moment experience.

There's a trap here, however, in terms of thinking. Figuring out what really adds value to your life, what's really interesting and worth learning, often gets confused with what's easiest, most pressing, or most entertaining. That's how any of us, no matter how smart we are, can get hooked on substitutes for learning that become bad habits and even addictions.

Technical traps like TV, video games, or cell phone apps; compulsive traps like eating, sex, shopping, working, procrastinating; or more dangerous traps such as bingeing and purging, gambling, or drinking and drugs; these begin with pleasure, but can become false values. Playing video games and drinking a beer aren't wrong until they become what we think about all the time. They don't really express our true self, but we can easily think they do. Escapist habits, compulsions, and addictions all have a common denominator—they begin as a pleasant way to mask the alarm, and ultimately, they produce even more stress.

What's missing when thinking gets sidetracked by habit, compulsion, or addiction? Or when life seems totally blah because we've forgotten to ask ourselves what gives our lives meaning? Clear *thinking* about your core values, about what gives you a sense of being in the right place, on the right track, doing what you believe in, is what truly makes the world a better place for you to live in.

When you think about your core values, you optimize the partnership between the alarm and the learning brain. Instead of recalling thoughts that cause alarm emotions like anxiety and fear, under stress your brain recalls what you value most: thoughts that keep you focused on the experiences you enjoy.

## The Cat in the Hat

Theodor Geisel started writing and drawing cartoons at Dartmouth College in the early 1920s. He rose to the position of editor-in-chief of the college's humor magazine, the *Jack-O-Lantern*, before being thrown out for breaking the school's anti-prohibition laws. His punishment for throwing a drinking party with friends was removal from the magazine's staff, but he loved his art. His core value as a young man was creative work, so he didn't stop writing and drawing; he just changed his byline to Seuss.

After Dartmouth he worked toward his PhD at Oxford, hoping to satisfy his father's desire for him to be a professor. The work bored him, so he left short of his degree and returned to America. Just as Geisel kept writing and drawing at Dartmouth after being fired, the value of honoring his father was not as important to Geisel as the creative life. His brain sent an alarm signal when what he was doing didn't match what was important to him.

Geisel began publishing cartoons for magazines like the *Saturday Evening Post*. To support himself and his wife during the Great Depression, he worked in advertising. But still, he exercised his artistic love as he drew his ads for companies like General Electric and Standard Oil. On the side, in the mid-'30s, he began writing and illustrating children's books. His first, *And to Think That I Saw It on Mulberry Street*, was rejected more than three dozen times, but he loved his work and kept trying to find it a publisher until Vanguard bought and released it in 1937.

Wanting to support his country during World War II, he put aside his work on children's books. In addition to his art, Geisel was an opinionated activist, and he supported President Roosevelt and the president's belief in the war. He drew for the Treasury department and even joined the Army as captain of its animation department. As celebrities like Charles Lindbergh opposed America's involvement in the war, Geisel had no problem drawing the flying hero as an Ostrich. He used his talent to train the troops as well, creating a series featuring a character, Private Snafu, whose bumblings became one of the most successful ways to warn enlisted men about the perils of battle. In both cases, whether to defend or strengthen the war effort, he used his love of drawing to live out another core belief: the importance of America engaging in the Great War.

When the war ended, he moved to California and returned to children's books. In 1954, he got his chance to combine his love of drawing and his penchant for strong opinions in a seminal project. He read an article in *Life* magazine about the increasing problem of childhood literacy in America. Plain and simple: boring reading primers weren't inspiring kids to learn. So Geisel, writing under the pseudonym Dr. Seuss, wrote *The Cat in the Hat* using 223 of the 348 words that every six-year-old was expected to know.

When he put his core values behind his work, he began a series of reading primers like *Green Eggs and Ham* and *The Grinch Who Stole Christmas*. Today, over 222 million of his books are in print, and hundreds of millions of children have learned to read because of what he loved to think about. Geisel never had children. Some reports say he didn't even like spending time with children. But he loved his art and he loved making a difference through witty drawing and word play.

What did Dr. Seuss discover that clear thinking makes possible for each of us?

## Core Values and the Brain

We discover our core values throughout our lives by reflecting on the experiences that are most important to us and turning what's meaningful into the thoughts we live by. They emerge over time. Dr. Seuss didn't know at Dartmouth that he was going to teach the world to read. He loved to draw and had deep convictions, but realizing what he loved to focus his thinking on was not as simple as just saying, "I'll just grab the first thought that comes to mind and think that because it's easy." If that was the case, he might have stopped drawing when he was kicked off the magazine. He didn't make his core value the first thing he was told to believe or he would have become a professor like his father wanted.

You can't grab the first thought if you want to exercise the thinking center's ability to learn. When your alarm tells your thinking center what it "should be" thinking, or when we try to live up to what other people have told us is "right," that's when our thoughts can spin or freeze. When the brain is in survival mode, the stressed-out thoughts that result are reactive attempts by the alarm to stop us from experiencing something that could hurt us physically or emotionally.

So where do our thoughts come from? Thinking begins with sensing and feeling. The five senses that enable our bodies to survive and thrive in any physical environment also provide information that flows into our minds like we're watching five movies at once. The first thing the body does with this information, after making automatic adjustments that are controlled by the reptile brain, is to channel it chemically and electrically to the emotional and learning brain.

The brain organizes the flood of sensory input into a set of files. These files take the form of chemical reactions and electrical pulses that we experience as ideas.

Different areas of the brain participate in different ways in translating sensory data into ideas. The brain areas that we've focused on in understanding stress reactions are by no means the only ones involved in thinking, but they are the stars in the show.

The alarm creates physical feelings, which become emotion, and brain scientists have found that emotion mixed with thought leaves a lasting impression on our lives and in our memories. Emotionally charged thoughts are strong and sticky. They capture our attention and hold it, even when we'd rather not have a particular thought. On a mundane level, this happens when we can't get a song out of our heads or a certain commercial makes us want to buy cookies every time we go to the grocery store.

A more serious example is when someone says something that hurts us and we can't forget her words, or we have a traumatic experience, and that causes us to think we're worthless, even though the experience is long in the past. Thankfully, emotionally charged thoughts can also be positive: the kind of ideas that inspire us for a lifetime after hearing a moving speech or helping someone else do something important to him or her.

But when does conscious thinking come into the picture? That might seem obvious: it must be when the brain's thinking center gets those emotional impulses and shapes them into intelligent thoughts. Correct, but before the thinking center can get into the act, it needs more than sensory and emotional information. It needs words.

Words are the mind's way of expressing what the body senses and the emotional brain feels. Words don't come from the brain's thinking center; they come from the combined efforts of many parts of the emotional and the learning brain. However, the key player is the brain's memory center.

The memory center communicates with areas throughout the cortex like a librarian collecting books from the stacks. This information is not yet in the form of words; rather, it is memories that aren't completely spelled out. You know when this happens in your brain: you can feel an intuitive sense that you know something, but you can't quite find the words to express it. What brain science tells us is that when we search for an idea, the memory center goes looking for information by retrieving bits and pieces of files stored all over the brain. When we don't yet know what we think, this search is directed by the alarm and reward centers, which tell the memory center to get information about possible problems or pleasures.

The files that the memory center pulls up when we try to figure out what's going on, before we've sorted out our thoughts, are selected based upon emotions generated by the alarm and reward centers. If your alarm signals you to feel impatient, bored, sad, anxious, or angry, you'll tend to remember things and people and situations that made you feel that way in the past. If your reward center is getting positive input and you're feeling happy and satisfied, you'll tend to remember other experiences or thoughts that you associate with those more pleasant emotions.

Except for one little twist. If the reward center is not getting the chemical input that it depends upon—primarily based on the brain chemical dopamine—it can trigger the alarm. That's when you have a powerful alarm reaction such as an intense craving. What's more, the alarm almost always tends to trump the reward center if both are pulling memories. If your alarm sends out a message of boredom and frustration, even though your reward center wants you to get some excitement in your life, your memory center is more likely to pull up files of boredom or frustration than excitement or pleasure.

So alarm signals will almost always shape the first thoughts that come to mind—especially when you're feeling stressed. But they're really not fully formed thoughts yet—they're leftover memories. And the memories aren't necessarily what you really think at that moment; they're *past thoughts* that fit with what your alarm feels right now. Technically, *you haven't even started to actually think yet*. You're running on emotion and memories that fit the feeling of that moment. This explains why we tend to repeat the past. We're reactively remembering rather than proactively thinking, and thus, not thinking clearly or creatively.

But the story doesn't have to end here. The brain has a thinking center for a reason. Just as emotions can be separated into two categories, alarm and optimal, the same is true of thoughts. Alarm thoughts are relatively fixed and inflexible because they are leftover memories from past problems or dangers. Not surprisingly, therefore, alarm thoughts are what trigger your brain to continue pumping adrenaline into your body, causing the physical experience of stress, and the potential of a meltdown. Optimal thoughts, on the other hand, are those that express your core values and open up communication between your thinking center and your alarm.

When you activate your thinking center to separate what kind of thought your brain is producing, you raise your level of personal control. When you figure out what your optimal thought is, you turn down your alarm because the alarm knows you know what really matters in the present moment. Discovering your optimal thoughts, which are your core values, may not happen instantly. What we can't forget though, is that if you keep thinking about what's most important, you eventually will.

## Escalation

The reason too many of us drown in negative thoughts is that we live as prisoners of our reptile and emotional brains. We heard this story from one of our clients who was learning to reduce her mood swings at the end of long, busy days.

When Emily got home from work, she was always tired and hungry, but also so excited to be with her family. Her husband, a stay-at-home dad, called her on the way home one day to say he'd made her favorite dinner. She had an optimal thought: "He really loves me."

As she got out of the car, she grabbed her coffee cup from the morning. She lifted her purse off the driver seat floor. She got out and opened the back door to grab her briefcase and the dry-cleaning she picked up on the way. Then, as she turned to close the door, her purse slipped from her shoulder. It dropped abruptly onto her elbow, catapulting her mug into the air. It flipped end over end, landing with a Bang! on the concrete floor.

The mug was metal so it might not even have dented, but that didn't stop Emily's alarm from firing. At first she had a mild alarm emotion: irritation. But then the trouble boiled as she had a thought. "If my husband only had a job, my life wouldn't be so stressful." Then her typical reaction happened. Intense alarm emotion ripped through her body. She felt completely angry, ready to throw her purse. Moments before she had been truly happy, grateful to be home and see her family, and totally in love with her wonderful husband. Now, suddenly, Emily was a wreck, ready to tell him what a failure she thought he was.

This is a perfect example of how an alarm thought can take us from a calm, happy state to an emotional flood such as feeling enraged, defeated, or disgusted. It's also the moment we have to draw on our core values. Even when everything is or feels like it's falling apart, Emily still loves her family. At the end of a long day, the mug incident immediately reveals that she is exhausted. Her reptile brain screams for food and her alarm screams thoughts about what needs to be different so she's safe. But there is a good reason she's exhausted: her family.

In these moments we can do an SOS by stepping back and orienting to the simple thought, "I love my family." The last thing you want to do is go into the house with fire shooting from your eyes. You can't say to yourself, "Don't be angry." You should be angry: you're tired, hungry, and your life is hard sometimes. But you can stop the flood by stepping back and orienting to the thought, "I love my family."

Those words ignite your learning brain. Now your thinking center knows what you need: thoughts, feelings, and images showing how precious your family members are to you. That simple knowledge empowers your thinking center to send an immediate request to your memory center to search the brain for precisely those thoughts, feelings, and images. You may still need to deal with feelings and thoughts generated by your alarm, but now you'll have the strength and support of a core value—your love for your family—to help you to feel hope, think clearly, and make the best decisions, instead of just feeling stressed.

If you complete the SOS with a self-check and your level of personal control is lower than you need, that doesn't mean that that core value didn't work. Nor does it mean that you didn't do a good enough job of picking or orienting your mind to that core value. It simply means you need to take more time—possibly only a few minutes, but sometimes longer—to fully focus your thinking center on that core value. Or it may be that you have other core values that are equally or even more important to you at this moment, and you may need to exercise more than one core value to achieve the sense of personal control that you seek.

Remember, it's not what you "do" in the sense of dealing directly with a stressful challenge that optimizes your personal control. It's what you *choose as your guiding thoughts* that can give you genuine personal control. When you're guided by your core values, you may still be feeling a high degree of stress (if your alarm continues to tell you there is a problem or a threat), but you have the certainty of knowing that whatever you choose to do will be a way of not only dealing with stress but also living your core values.

While our client wasn't able to turn down her stress the first few times she used an SOS to orient to her core values, she didn't give up. That would have been an unfortunate alarm reaction, not an optimal choice. Instead, with consistent focus on thoughts about what mattered most to her, in a few weeks, as quickly as her stress reactions came up, her sense of personal control kicked in and her alarm calmed down and allowed the stress reactions to recede.

Each time she entered the garage, she thought about the dinner she was about to share with her husband and kids. In that moment, no matter how strong the stress reaction she was feeling, she'd think, "I love my family." Enough exercising of that core value, and it became the guiding focus and source of calm for her every night. She wasn't free of stress reactions, but she had something new that enabled her to do more than just grit her teeth and cope with the distress signals from her alarm. She knew that she could always choose, no matter how strong the alarm reaction, to focus on what she wanted to think about.

## The Practice of Exercising Core Values

You see famous artists, business people, and public servants exercising their core values every day. But they didn't start out famous, and they fortified what they truly believe over time. Mother Teresa left the convent and worked with the poor in the streets of Calcutta because she felt she had to live among those in need. She wasn't famous then. Her alarm must have screamed at the stress of helping so many hurting people. As she did so much good, she attracted the press. She was criticized and scrutinized at the end of her life for the condition of her orphanages and the way she handled donations. But she didn't stop. She continued to focus on helping the poor, and four thousand monks and nuns continue her work today.

Another example of the results of exercising core values comes from the experience of John Melia of Roanoke, Virginia. With family and friends, he founded the Wounded Warrior Project in 2002. John was severely injured in a 1992 helicopter accident in Somalia. He wanted to make sure the gap between the needs of wounded vets and what the government provides would be filled. Today, his organization has helped thousands of servicemen and servicewomen reclaim their lives after the physical and psychological traumas of war.

Like tens of thousands of other military combat veterans, Melia experienced the onslaught of extreme stress reactions normal to the shock and horror of war. He recognized that war is physically and emotionally wounding to soldiers, and he dedicated himself to helping warriors to heal from those wounds. Instead of allowing his wounds to take his life and his personal control away from him, he exercised his core values:

loyalty to his fellow soldiers and the duty to bring them hope. This is how exercising core values offers people a sense of peace and how, out of stress, we can make invaluable contributions to those around us.

Alarm thoughts not only aren't bad or a problem, they also aren't opposed to optimal thoughts. Alarm thoughts are an essential part of optimal thoughts. Alarm thoughts can actually point us toward core values beyond safety and survival, providing insightful evidence about the other core values that we really care about. The alarm fills us with thoughts not only to keep us out of trouble, but also to tell us when what we think does not match what we truly believe. Worrying if we can trust someone, for instance, is actually quite helpful. It reminds us to think: is this person really interested in me? Will they actually be the kind of person I can trust? And that thinking and paying attention is a way to waken ourselves and open new options in our lives.

Like the Five Pillars of Islam or the Ten Commandments of the Judeo-Christian faith, each of us has more than one belief that rules our lives. But there is usually one value that trumps all the others. We want you to identify it now as you begin to learn how to exercise core values, because if you don't know what truly drives your life, it's easy for the confusion to pull you pack into alarm world.

On a piece of paper, list five values that define you. These are the beliefs—ideas, places, people—that are most precious to you.

When we ask this of clients or in our research, we most often hear family. We want our families to be safe, strong, and supported. And yet the very same people who want their families to be happy and healthy struggle with addiction or abuse issues, and often choose their work or some other interest over spending time with their families. It's easy to end up in alarm world when the pressures and pace of modern life trigger us.

And, for every thought that triggers you, there is also an optimal thought in the background that expresses what you think and most deeply believe at your core. When you can identify these thoughts among your alarm thoughts, that's when you feel in control. That's when you feel your life is worth living.

Look at your list again. Another way to consider what makes up your core values is to wonder which of these values you'd sacrifice the most for. For which value would you work twenty hours a day? For which value would you give all your money? For which value would you give your life?

We're pushing you to think in these extreme ways because we want you to recognize that there is something in your life so important that even risking your life wouldn't cause you to melt down. Your thinking center can always see you through the danger—as long as your thoughts and choices are guided by the core values that empower your thinking center. When core values are your guide, this enables your thinking center to partner with your alarm so that you can think clearly enough to feel—and *be*—in control, even when your body is pumping adrenaline and turning on all the survival systems that the alarm activates.

When we focus on the value that matters most to us, we aren't at the mercy of our stress reactions. The athlete who survives the pressure of the moment, the parent who takes care of his sick child and at the same time does amazing work, the doctor who performs critical surgery in a life or death situation, the teacher who can inspire, even during the last of seven classes that day: these are examples of people exercising their core values in the midst of real stress. Even when their alarms send messages that cause stress, they can still model the ideas that are most important to their lives.

What is your deepest core value?

Circle it.

Now do an SOS. Step back. Orient on that idea. Where is your stress level? Where is your level of personal control?

When we think about how much we love our kids, or focus on freedom, when we think about improving our community or enjoying the work we do, our alarm turns down. The alarm turns down when it knows that what is most important to us is at the center of our mind—that's when it doesn't have anything to worry about.

Under extreme stress, it is usually impossible to instantly recall an optimal thought that will counteract an alarm thought like, "I'm a failure." The trick to exercising your core values is to clearly define them during periods of reflection when you're not stressed. This way, when you find yourself in alarm world, your brain has clear categories of thought to draw on instead of thoughts that cause you to cycle back into negative emotions and the unhealthy choices we all can make. When you know your core values, you can stay focused on what matters to you even in stressful times.

## Why Doesn't Positive Thinking Always Work?

If you're not feeling positive, the worst thing you can do for your alarm is to try to make yourself think a "positive" thought. At that moment, it just doesn't ring true to try to think, "I love my life." If you've just gotten a painful health diagnosis, lost a job, or broken up with someone you love, your alarm is triggered. It doesn't want you to get hurt, so when you are suffering, or feeling pain, it floods you with chemicals so you remember that you really don't want to feel this way again.

When we try to tell our brains that everything is fine, in clear resistance to the obvious signals that we're in trouble, they will work harder to keep us safer. They know we can't control all the circumstances that surround us so they're going to protect us, even from ourselves. The result: the more positive we try to "think" in the face of negative experience, the worse we feel.

Positive thinking only works if the positive thought is a genuine statement of a core value. Remember, to get to the step of exercising your core values, you must first recognize the alarm emotions and thoughts that are a sign that you're having a stress reaction, as well as the trigger(s) that are setting off your alarm. Then, the positive thinking has to be more than just a wish or faint hope.

Positive thoughts often fail to help us feel happier, calmer, or more in control because they are negative (alarm) thoughts in disguise. For example, take the thought, "What's most important to me right now is to get out of this mess!" It's phrased as an optimal thought ("what's most important to me"), but it really is an alarm thought. It's all about coping with or surviving a problem, not about what makes life meaningful and worthwhile. The goal of an alarm thought is safety and relief. The goal of an optimal thought is what gives your life value and what you value most in life.

In order to exercise your core values, the thoughts that you focus on have to be framed in terms of what you really care about. In the middle of a health scare, "I'm going to be fine" won't turn down the alarm, but something like "I trust my doctors to help me heal" can. If you lose your job, saying, "I'll get another one" may cause you more stress, while thinking, "I look forward to the challenge of finding a new place to use my skills" could help. Obviously if you don't trust your doctors, or you hate the thought of a job search, these aren't the right ideas. They are, however, examples of the kind of creative thinking you have to do to turn down your alarm.

The mock self-help guru from *Saturday Night Live*, Stuart Smalley, used to say at the end of his show, "I'm good enough, I'm smart enough, and doggone it, people like me!" It was so funny because usually we're not good enough, smart enough, or well enough liked to do some of the things we really want to do—but we can be.

Effective positive thinking focuses on what's most important in the optimal sense, not what alarms you or what you think you need to avoid, escape, or fix. And positive thinking is most valuable when we're thinking about the goals that drive our daily experience.

Differentiating alarm and optimal goals is the next way to focus your brain.

# Chapter Eleven

# Determine Your Optimal Goals

The third way we'll work on focusing using SOS involves paying attention to your goals. By paying attention to your goals many times each day—not just when you have the space and time to reflect—you can choose the experiences of your life. The brain's alarm doesn't know to stop and think before reacting. For instance, if a bear chases you, the alarm sends a signal that forces you to either run away or play dead. The alarm just wants you to be safe. Survivalists recommend playing dead if it's a grizzly and rising to your full height and acting like a stronger animal if you run into a black or brown bear. But who has time to think about what kind of bear is chasing you when it's happening? React the wrong way and the results can be perilous.

Our goals quickly form out of the pressures and demands of the immediate moment. And that's the problem: stress causes most of us to put what we really want aside until we alleviate whatever created the stress. Instead of living based on what's most important, our goals focus on survival. Facing immediate jeopardy, survival is good. Most of the time, we want more from life than to simply survive.

You empower your emotions by paying attention to both alarm and optimal emotions. You exercise your core values by paying attention to alarm thoughts and then focusing on thoughts that reflect what's most important to you in your life. The "D" in FREEDOM represents the need to *determine your optimal goals.*

# What Is a Goal?

*A goal is what you need in order to feel fulfilled in your life.* Goals can be personal or they can be communal. They can be something you want to experience day after day or a height you want to reach over time. They can be a feeling, an object, a relationship, or an idea. In every case, a goal is the tangible statement of something you hope to achieve in the future and that you're willing to commit time and energy to pursue.

Goals, like emotions and thoughts, fall into two categories: reactive, alarm goals and focused, optimal goals. Every emotion and thought leads to a goal, whether we're aware of it or not. When you focus your mind using SOS, your goals will be a combination of what your alarm is seeking (safety, security, problems solved) and the accomplishments and achievements that you seek because of what you need to feel and your core values.

A perfect example of an alarm goal can be found in childhood: when we were children, almost all of us at one time said, "I'm running away and I'm never coming back." The conflict that turned on our alarms may have been as simple as eating a cookie when we shouldn't have, or as serious as real trauma in our household, but our reactive goal was the same: I'm starting a new life away from all this madness.

When you realize a goal is reactive, it turns on the thinking center. You may still be reacting emotionally, but you've focused your thinking center on deciding whether you're ultimately going to make your choice based on survival or on an optimal life. The core of everything we're teaching you is to open up the pathway between the learning brain and the survival brain. The moment you recognize that a goal creates a stress response, you have the opportunity to emphasize a different goal that is optimal.

Your optimal goals, the hopes and dreams you pursue to build the life that matters most to you, do not flood your system with adrenaline when you focus on them. That doesn't mean if you're a mountain climber or a race-car driver, the activity itself won't engage your survival brain; but when you think about what you need, optimal goals create a high level of personal control, which keeps you centered even with adrenaline in your system. To be centered is to know that what you're experiencing right now, even if it is uncomfortable, is worth experiencing.

## Reaching the Top of the World: Mount Everest, Part II

In 1982, Mark Inglis and his climbing partner Phil Doole were trapped in an ice cave on Aoraki, also known as Mount Cook. The mountain with two names—the first, given by the native New Zealanders, means "cloud piercer," while Cook came from the English in honor of their first Captain to survey New Zealand—is the highest in New Zealand. A freak series of storms trapped Inglis and Doole for more than thirteen days.

Inglis had dreamed of being a climber since childhood. At age eleven he set the goal of climbing Mount Everest. He began his career as a search-and-rescue mountaineer in 1979 at age twenty. When people ask him why he became a climber, he playfully says, "I sucked at rugby. Nothing else to do in New Zealand." Like the fellow New Zealander and first climber to ever reach the summit of Everest, Sir Edmund Hillary, Inglis wanted to climb for the rest of his life with the world's highest peak as his optimal goal.

When Inglis and Doole were rescued, both climbers knew they had some frostbite. They expected to lose some of their toes, and counted themselves lucky. But a month later, Inglis went into surgery the day before Christmas. He woke up Christmas morning without his legs below the knee. Imagine his alarm that next day. All he had wanted to do with his life was climb, and now, he had lost his legs.

In the years that followed, he became a winemaker and a skier. He won a silver medal on his bicycle in the 2000 Paralympic Games. But it wasn't enough. He could never bury the optimal goal that had been his focus since he was eleven. With incredible training and preparation, twenty-four years later, on May 15, 2006, he became the first ever double amputee to summit Mount Everest.

How would a goal drive a person for twenty-four years to train, experiment with equipment, and then deal with unimaginable challenges before and during the climb? The climb of Everest would take forty days in total. On one of the lower parts of the climb, one of his prosthetic legs broke during a fall. He repaired it with duct tape while a spare was brought from base camp.

Optimal goals enable us to take all the information from our alarms, even incredible pain and real danger, and keep focusing on what we need to experience to be whole and to live a life of value. A truly focused mind can use the adrenaline and power of the alarm, capable of lifting cars off a child, to do what seems impossible.

As recounted in *Everest: Beyond the Limit*, the documentary about Inglis's climb, Inglis and his team even encountered another climber who would ultimately perish on Everest that day. Exhausted and oxygen deprived, their alarms couldn't help but scream. But Inglis's goal was so clear that, even as he climbed past places where others had died, he was able to keep going. Any brain would have screamed that what he was doing was crazy, but he had a goal that had guided him since childhood, and it took him to the top of the world.

## Goals and the Brain

*What is the purpose of goals?*

The usual answer, and it is good common sense, is that goals are good because they enable us to organize our lives and achieve our potential as human beings. But our short answer is a little different and not what you'd expect. From the perspective of our brains, personal goals define who we are. *Our goals are our identity.* And when we think and act based upon goals that reflect our core values as well as what we have to deal with due to life's stresses, we create an identity for ourselves that can withstand any stressor.

Without goals, we are simply our reptile and emotional brain reacting to our surroundings. That's the reason teenagers try on different identities like costumes. In the development from adolescence to adulthood, it is our deepest personal goals that become the core files in our memory center that drive the development of our learning brains. Adults have more defined identities. They may evolve or change over time, but the goals of our lives don't rearrange with every new person we meet or challenge we face. This core identity, or self, is based on our fundamental values that become goals, and it guides us in what we focus on every day.

An identity based on alarm goals will almost always lead to stress. Alarm goals don't guide us toward whom we need to be in our lives, they push us toward what we feel we have to do in order to escape a problem or satisfy an addiction. Alarm goals lead us to define ourselves in terms of temporary satisfaction or chronic problems, both of which are a recipe for feeling not only stressed, but fundamentally incomplete and unfulfilled.

For example, say your life revolved around watching a particular television show, or following the events in a celebrity's life. What might have been a healthy initial interest in the show or person could become an obsession. That's an extreme alarm goal. In fact, all addictions are the product of an alarm goal that has grown to the point that the alarm takes over our life. The craving or obsession comes to define our identity.

Feeling like we *have to* have something or *have to* get away from someone or something is the first clue to determining if we're caught in the revolving door that alarm goals always create. That's our alarm dictating our goals, and the harder we try to accomplish that goal the more stress we feel. That's why achieving alarm goals is often unsatisfying. They're not really about what we need and value in life, but instead about getting something we don't have or getting away from something we fear.

One way to think about alarm and optimal goals is what Margaret Atwood described as the difference between "freedom from" and "freedom to." What she meant was that when our goals are to get away or be safe from something, we're always on the defensive. On the other hand, when we're free to pursue what we truly value, we're free. That's when we can move beyond just avoiding pain and seeking pleasure.

Optimal goals lead us toward who we are and can be in our lives. Optimal goals are an expression of the beliefs, values, and hopes that are, as Abraham Lincoln said, "the better angels of our nature." A life oriented toward optimal goals is not necessarily a stress-free or error-free life, but it is a life that you can look back on at the end of the day or the end of the road with a sense of it having been worth it.

Focusing more often and more regularly on the goals that reflect what we truly value, we provide our thinking and memory centers with a chance to counterbalance the pressures that come from alarm goals— while still honoring the intent of our brain's alarm to protect us and help us get immediate rewards as well. For example, an optimal goal might be as mundane (but still important) as enjoying the taste of our favorite food, or as deep as giving our child the chance to be whoever they want to be.

An identity defined by optimal goals not only grounds us in what we do and how other people think and feel about us, but also focuses us on what we know to be true and important in life. That is different for each of us, but it is a possible reality for all of us.

## Long-Term and Immediate Goals

Let's say you want to become a chef whose restaurant earns a Michelin star. It's one of the highest honors to have this guide, begun in 1900, proclaim your food to be the best in the world. But at this moment you cook macaroni and cheese from a box. You watched a cooking show, were excited by the idea of centering your life around food, and decided to become a master chef. You tested the idea by taking a few cooking classes. After really testing the idea for a few years, by cooking almost every recipe in the *Joy of Cooking*, it keeps nagging at you. You are ready to give up your present job and cook professionally. You still want to create a restaurant that earns a Michelin star. That restaurant is a long-term goal.

For a singer, the long-term goal might be performing at the Metropolitan Opera. For a baseball player, making it to the major leagues.

For a professor, earning tenure. For a writer, publishing a book. The long-term goals we create are the mountaintops that drive us. They are the experience we want in the future. They do not raise our alarms when we dream of these goals; they are the pleasant place our mind can wander, experiencing a sample of the pleasure we'll feel when we accomplish something extraordinary.

Our long-term goals usually combine both the fears of our alarms and the core values that guide our thinking centers. At first, you may be mainly aware of the values that your long-term goals embody. But don't be surprised when, and it can come on suddenly, your alarm starts sending anxious messages wondering if you'll ever get there. Our alarms don't want us to fail, and instead of feeling excitement about the future, they can push us to feel worry or even horror about what will prevent us from reaching our dreams.

Which is why we also need immediate goals. The great chefs begin their training doing the simplest of exercises over and over: knife skills, basic sauces, cooking meat and eggs to an exact level of doneness. If they focused on getting a Michelin star while julienning carrots, they might lose a finger. If in the middle of their first job, they talked about the honors they would receive as a chef rather than creating perfect dishes as a line cook, they would never internalize the technique and artistic vision necessary to be great one day.

Immediate goals are what keep us focused on the present, and allow our alarms to stay under control. They include the input from the alarm, to keep us safe and alert to immediate opportunities, but they also include what's most important to us in life. In every immediate goal there is a wealth of deeper values and hopes that are our long-term goals—if we take the time to look closely. They point directly to what we truly need in the future.

## Why It's Difficult to Delay Gratification

As we focus on our immediate goals to fulfill our long-term hopes, our brains can make it hard to delay gratification. Researchers have known for decades what human beings have known for millennia: given the choice between a smaller immediate reward and a larger delayed reward, almost always, we pick the quick fix. This can be the smart choice. Why wait for something you might never get when you can be sure of getting something right now?

What's the difference between the dedicated individual who perseveres in seeking the larger delayed gratification and the rest of us for whom immediate gratification seems so compelling and irresistible? Genetics and inborn personality may play a role, but research has shown that the key to delaying immediate gratification is the awareness of the larger rewards.

In laboratory studies, when psychologists offer rats small immediate rewards such as a sip of sugar water or a pellet of food, they will choose that immediate gratification over a larger delayed reward *except* when they are reminded frequently of the larger reward. When they learn that a certain cue, such as a light turning on in their cage, signals that the larger reward is available, they will stop hunting for the smaller rewards and do whatever they have to for as long as it takes in order to get the larger delayed reward.

We have more personal control than animals, most of the time. But what we fail to do is remember the larger rewards in our life. We either do what's easier and more pleasurable, even though it won't get us closer to what we really need, or our brains live so alarmed that all we can do each day is get away from the things that threaten us or cause us pain. What turns on that light for us, so that we remember that there's more to life than the temporary sources of relief or minor gratifications right in front of us?

The key to focusing on our optimal goals, whether immediate or long-term, is the interplay of the alarm, memory center, and thinking center. Impulsive choices, such as drinking too much to deal with problems at work, originate in the brain's alarm.

For the alarm, any delay is too long to wait. Remember, the alarm operates in an eternal *now* because it doesn't know the difference between past, present, and future. If the reward center identifies something that seems either desirable or undesirable, it signals the alarm to send the body a wake-up call. If it's a reward that will calm the alarm, the alarm wants it desperately and immediately even if what we're about to do is in conflict with our optimal goals.

The alternative is to determine your optimal goals and focus on them intentionally. A brain focused on an optimal goal turns down the impulsive messages from the reward center and the alarm. When your thinking center knows what is most important to you, it's like a lightbulb going off above your head. What you want reactively suddenly becomes less important than what you want ultimately.

## The Practice of Differentiating Alarm and Optimal Goals

You may have thought that SOS was useful primarily to sort out your emotions and thoughts, but that's just the start. Knowing the difference between alarm and optimal emotions and thoughts prepares you to take the next crucial step: translating those feelings and thoughts into goals.

Optimal goals are based upon *needs* not *wants*. Most of us want to be a millionaire (or, these days, a billionaire). But we need more than a pile of money. We need security, accomplishment, and fulfillment. Money can seem like a guarantee of happiness or respect, when in reality it is just the facilitator for reaching optimal goals like happiness or respect.

Optimal goals are rewards or accomplishments that we look back on with satisfaction. Determining your optimal goals is possible when you do an SOS using a specific question: what do I need *that I already have* that makes my life complete and worth living?

Let's try it. Remember, practicing SOS when you're not stressed is how your brain learns to deal with stress naturally when your alarm sounds.

First, step back. Take a few deep breaths or close your eyes and listen. Now focus on that thing that you have that gives your life value. What thought did you orient to?

Two kinds of goals emerge. Your alarm will create goals like, "I need to be popular" or "I need to be smarter or more successful than other people." If your goal was, "I need to get out of this job, or relationship," these are important goals to consider, but they are what's missing or wrong in your life. They are alarm goals, not what's important to you.

Sweep your mind clear again. Refocus on what's really important to you *that you already have*. Optimal goals give you a sense of happiness, self-respect, confidence, and hope. Optimal goals are what you have that already makes your life precious. Focus on *what you need more of that you already have*. Time, room to practice, a slower pace—pick one thing that enriches your life:

- a relationship with someone for whom, and from whom, you feel a deep sense of love or friendship or respect
- something you love to do because you feel absorbed and interested while doing it and afterward you feel a sense of accomplishment and satisfaction
- something in nature, the arts, or sports that, when you see or hear it, gives you a deep sense of pleasure and completion

After orienting to that optimal goal, notice what happens to your stress level, on the scale of one to ten; now notice what happens to your sense of personal control, on the scale of one to ten. Stress may or may not change, but control always goes up, even if only a little, when you clear your mind and fully focus on an optimal goal. That's because you've activated your brain's thinking center in the most powerful and complete way possible.

You've integrated emotion, thought, and goals into a statement of what you most deeply believe in. By using SOS to bring that optimal goal into focus, you shine the light on your true identity. You're activating your memory center to not only find that goal but to make it more prominent and easier to access when you need it in the future.

Do this kind of SOS regularly, and you know who you are. You prime your brain to do two new things when your alarm goes off. First, the alarm signal will activate your thinking center. How will you know that? Because in the beginning you'll find yourself thinking, "I know my alarm is triggered, and that's telling me to pay attention to what I need as well as what I want." After enough time doing SOS, it happens naturally, and you'll think, "What do I need to focus on right now, so that I'm guided by what's really important to me in my life?"

Second, your thinking center will activate your memory center. In the past, it was the alarm that typically activated your memory center. That's why stressful feelings, images, and ideas too often dominated what was on your mind. The thinking center couldn't step in to help the memory center get unstuck from alarm files, and enable it to search for and find memories that are based on your optimal feelings, thoughts, and goals.

But now you know that focusing on an optimal goal, *what you already have in your life that makes your life feel right and worth living*, is the way to get the thinking center to step in and balance the demands of the alarm with a stronger message to the memory center: find what I know that isn't just about problems or survival. Your optimal goal allows your memory center to pull the files you need right now in order to feel calm and confident. That's what helps you make the right choices for yourself and for the people you care about, even when you're stressed.

Focusing on your optimal goals every day, several times a day, using SOS, can make the difference between being trapped by stress and what the alarm wants you do, and being free from stress because you are paying attention to what you need—and how you already fulfill those needs. The skill is to consciously use your thinking center and memory center so you know it.

## There Is an Optimal Goal in Every Alarm Goal

In every alarm reaction, there is an optimal goal as well as an alarm goal. For example, your child runs out into the street. This triggers your alarm.

In that moment, you do not think about your long-term goal of raising a compassionate world citizen. You have an immediate alarm goal: keep him safe. You do anything you can to get him out of harm's way.

What you do next, however, is based on your optimal goal of raising an intelligent, caring human being. With your body flooded with adrenaline, even though your child is now safe, you may want to lash out or yell at him. That's an alarm reaction becoming hyperactive.

Once your child is out of danger, if you have a clear optimal goal you've thought about ahead of time—like wanting your child to grow up knowing how to be kind to others—the goal directs your brain to behave in a way that focuses your attention on what's most important.

Instead of spanking or screaming, you firmly tell the child to never go into the street without holding your hand and make sure he understands you. You remind him of this a few times that day so he doesn't forget, but you don't let your alarm cause you to react, even though the situation caused you stress.

We focus on our optimal goals because we don't want to live in alarm world. The difference between having a secure identity and feeling bad about ourselves is spending enough time identifying what we really need, even in situations that trigger us. Most people never take the time because they don't realize they can have an optimal life.

# Part IV

## An Optimal Life

# *Chapter Twelve*

# Optimize Your Choices

Everything you've learned so far about how your brain works, how to focus, and what you can focus on to turn down your alarm has shown you that you can always regain control of your life. When your alarm fires, or if it's been hyperactive for too long, it can feel like you're helpless. But you are stronger than you've ever known. You have options you've never been taught to look for. When we feel our alarm turning on, when we notice our bodies fill with stress, we can use SOS or recognize triggers to turn on our thinking center.

Something in your life right now is stressful. At work or with your family, in your immediate environment or a place you'll go later today: that situation, person, or place will cause your alarm to send stress through your body. Ultimately, it is a skill to balance the input from your alarm's stress reactions with the emotions, values, and goals that your thinking center brings into focus when you orient your mind to what's most important. It's a skill to choose to switch your focus. The "O" in the FREEDOM model is *optimize your choices*.

## Alarm Commands Keep Us Alive and Alert, but They Are Not Choices

You always have a choice. *Choice is the human freedom in each moment to decide the path of our lives.* Reactive alarm commands, however, are not choices. When your brain's alarm goes into survival mode, it demands that you defeat the enemy, escape the danger, or fix the problem. Alarm commands are not choices because they are about what you *have to* feel, think, want, or do. They may be the best course in a crisis, but they aren't actually choices because they haven't been informed by what you decide is most important in the moment or in your life.

When there is danger or a problem that can only be dealt with by fight, flight, or freezing, alarm commands may be the best "choice." Alarm commands are fast and strong, which are essential when threats or problems make the only choice survival.

When the alarm takes over and choices are replaced by commands, however, it can feel like we're completely at the mercy of things we can't control. Angry bosses, a bad economy, a neglectful spouse: the triggers that turn on our alarm and the thoughts and feelings that take over our brains and bodies can seem like a battle inside us we can't stop or win.

That kind of thinking can take over and lead you to see life as nothing more than a fight to be good rather than bad, or to be right instead of wrong. Those kinds of "black and white" or "all or nothing" views are the specialty of the alarm: from the perspective of the brain's alarm, you're either in danger or you're safe, damaged or fixed, powerless or in control. The alarm doesn't see options.

When stress reactions put us on automatic pilot, it strips us of the ability to make real choices. *But when the alarm, thinking, and memory centers are working together*, choice is not only possible, it is *inevitable*, even under the most extreme conditions of stress.

## Optimal Choices

You, the person you want to be, can step back whenever you feel stress reactions, and see that you don't just have to react to a situation. You have a choice the moment you stop and orient on what you want to learn. You can see the frantic phone call from a friend or the angry email from a coworker and decide the best way to help the person back from alarm world. Their alarms shut the door on the lives they would choose if they knew they had a choice.

You can be the kind of person who sees the opportunities in every mess, problem, or even threat. Even if that isn't your natural style, it can become the way that you make choices. For example, your child gets suspended. The immediate alarm reaction could be either to send your child to military school or to get irate at the school. What you do with that reaction depends on your awareness, both of your alarm and of the fact that you always have a choice in how you handle your alarm reactions.

People who live in alarm world react. They explode at their child or the child's teacher or principal. The person who chooses to live an optimal life knows that even this circumstance can be used to discover something meaningful for the child, the child's education, and an ongoing relationship with the school.

Optimal choices rarely are perfect or cost-free, but they don't have unacceptable downsides. If a choice has a lot of benefits but also has extreme costs, it is unlikely to be optimal. Yelling, or worse, at the principal won't help you or your child. It might feel better to release the anger at the moment, but the consequences of the choice will only create more alarm reactions. In almost every situation there is an optimal choice that will make learning possible.

Clearly, optimal choices require some thought. It's much easier to find a choice that is optimal when you're calm than when you're stressed. Ideally, we think through situations in advance when we have the time and composure to truly focus on what matters to us. It's much easier to think about what to say on a first date before the person is standing in front of you.

And, we all have times where we've made brilliant choices spontaneously or in the heat of a crisis. But most of those optimal choices *actually were already made in advance*, we just weren't aware we'd already thought about the situation before.

We can't anticipate every possible important choice, let alone the infinite number of smaller but potentially life-changing choices that will come up day-to-day. There is no way to script every key choice in advance. And even when a choice has been pre-scripted, it often needs adjustment at the moment to balance attaining what we value with the energy it takes to live an optimal life. What we can do is make sure we step back, even in the most ugly of circumstances, and think clearly enough to truly consider all our options.

## The Christmas Truce

In 1914, the trench warfare of World War I was unexplainably gruesome. Ten million would die and twice as many would be injured. Men, shoulder to shoulder, faced constant artillery shelling tearing up the land and churning up fields of mud and dead men. The invention of the machine gun, favored by the Germans, meant that every assault to advance the line caused instant casualties. The constant explosions, filth, and cold made it the worst of human life thrown on the shoulders of young men. The percentage of men who lost their lives on the Western front was double that of those who would fall in the same areas during WWII.

But something peculiar happened during Christmas week, 1914. To the dismay of their commanders, the men from opposite sides started celebrating together. At this early stage in the war, which had begun the previous summer, the poorly constructed trenches were as little as 30, 50, or 70 yards apart. It was possible for both sides to hurl insults as easily as they could lob mortar. The war had not progressed enough for the opposing forces to stop talking, so when Christmas packages of goodies from home and cigarettes and chocolate from the governments started arriving, happy soldiers changed their tunes from destruction to jubilation.

Stories vary as to what the Germans did to begin the truce, but it may have started with a chocolate cake and a note asking for a ceasefire. An embedded *British Daily Telegraph* reporter said the British accepted and offered tobacco as a confirming gift. At the appointed time, the Germans began to sing "Silent Night," placing candles on the sandbags protecting their trench. The Germans shouted for the Brits to join, but they replied, "We'd rather die than sing German." A German soldier retorted, "It would kill us if you did."

Word spread about the acts of generosity and humor, and the next day, the sounds of artillery and machine guns were lighter, and sometimes entirely silent. The Germans hoisted Christmas trees, decorated with lit candles, onto their parapets and for the next week, men sang throughout the day. For the week around Christmas and New Year's, it was not surprising to see soldiers from opposite sides mingling together in no man's land, and bringing gifts all the way to the enemy's trench.

In the most alarming of circumstances, what would cause these men to focus on the optimal world?

While our alarms try to keep us safe, our learning brains never stop trying to bring other options into our consciousness. No serviceman on either side wanted to spend Christmas in a flooded, stinking trench. Even though every alarm goal of their commanders would be to fight the enemy, the higher yearning of every human brain is for connection and the ability to be free of stress. When they realized it was possible to take control of the battlefield and live a better life even for a week, and live the best possible lives in that moment, they built their optimal world.

## Asking for Help

Devin had always been the superstar at work. She joined her advertising firm right out of college, and every year she had been given more and more responsibility. At twenty-nine, she was the youngest director the company had ever had. And, she was ready to quit.

In meetings, she tried to fake her usual enthusiasm. When she was with clients, she put on her normal charm and creatively worked their campaigns. But the same work that had made her the happiest among her friends now made her want a new life.

When Devin came to our office, we asked her to tell the story of when she started to feel stressed. She talked about one client that she just couldn't make happy. Everything her team did was wrong, even when it was exactly what the client had asked for. So she tried harder. She spent more hours than on any other piece of business. Her efforts helped retain the work and the client was still with her company. She hated working for them, but they were a huge part of her bottom line each year and the reason she was promoted.

We asked what her options were, and she said she didn't have any. We asked her about her favorite people at work, and her face brightened. She talked about her boss, one of the partners, whose office she could plop down in and talk about anything.

We asked if she'd talked about her feelings with him.

She said, "Of course not. I can't let him think I can't handle it. We complain about them, sure, but I can't ask for help."

We asked why not.

She said, "Because I don't want anything to get in the way of my becoming partner."

We asked if she did all her projects alone.

"Of course not," she said, and her eyes widened.

We asked if she thought the partner would see her as weak or strong if she asked for help dealing with a difficult client. We wondered out loud if it might not make the partner worry about her that she would keep what she really needed to herself when he'd made clear he wanted to help her.

She walked out of the office that day with a clear plan. We rehearsed ways to talk to the partner and did different SOS around the feelings, values, and goals that would keep her focused on getting what she needed, even though she was scared to ask for it.

At our next session, she told us that she chose to talk to him. The partner had always been amazed at how much she had been able to do and happily freed up more resources to help her. All she could talk about with us was how excited she was to love her work again.

# The Reactive Chain versus the Optimal Path

At work, at home, and even at war, what allows us to choose peace over violence, the value of human life and the goal of connection over victory and death?

When under stress, it is normal for feelings, both bodily and emotional, as well as our values and goals to be largely based on alarm reactions. A person whose boss yells at her instantly has a stress reaction. The thought that follows is something like, "This guy is an overpaid, loud-mouthed, orangutan." What comes next is an alarm goal like, "I've got to get out of here." The alarm choices that can naturally flow out of the reactive chain in this situation could be looking for another job, yelling back, or quitting.

People who follow the optimal path when they have alarm reactions take a different approach. When they feel a stress reaction coming, they step back. Before even doing an SOS, they notice that their bodies feel physically stressed, and they assess what emotions they're experiencing. That emotional awareness allows them to notice the alarm thoughts about their boss, and do an SOS on the myriad optimal thoughts that can turn down the emotional flood. With the stress turned down, instead of needing to get away, they choose an optimal goal such as understanding what caused the boss's reaction, or trying to rebuild the relationship. In this case, the optimal path leads to choices like finding a time to talk to the boss when he's calm, or asking for help from a colleague to figure out how to handle the situation differently next time. They may still consider the boss's reaction unacceptable and choose to seek another boss or job. However, they're doing it not as a reaction, but as a well-thought-out decision that increases rather than compromises their well-being and personal control. And in so doing, they reset the alarm instead of letting its reactions be the sole driver of their choices.

The soldiers in the Christmas Truce followed the optimal path. Their brains could so easily have been trapped by stress. The feeling of panic could have become the thought of violence, the goal of killing, and the actions that follow such intentions. What happened in their brains—the focus on feeling the warmth of the holidays, the thought of connection, and the goal of peace—allowed them to choose to celebrate rather than fight.

## Your Body Is a Temple

In every moment, we can choose to let the reactive chain take over our brains, or we can choose optimal actions based on the optimal world.

For instance, you are very tired and very hungry.

Just that sentence will trigger your alarm, and it should. The first human beings, who lived almost entirely from their alarms, had two main purposes: nourishment and safety. Remember Maslow's hierarchy of needs: your evolved self hasn't lost that primary set of demands on your daily life. So if you're late coming home from work, a situation made even worse by a quick workout that made you even hungrier, it doesn't matter that you may be driving in a luxury sedan or a comfortable family vehicle; your brain thinks you're in the ancient world. It wants food to sustain you and it wants it now.

You have two choices: the vegetables, soup, and fresh bread you made this weekend, just waiting in your fridge to fill your nutritional vacuum, or the gooey, hot, ready-in-seconds cheeseburger (insert whatever tempts you when your energy is low and you just want to feel better) available at the establishment you're about to drive by on the way home.

What do you normally choose?

Almost anyone would choose the immediate gratification provided by the burger (or whatever less than ideally healthy comfort food that you substituted). What's missing or wrong in this picture is that you're feeling too hungry or tired or stressed to focus your mind in the way we've just described. The very thought of doing an extended SOS at that moment probably seems absurd, or at least like a form of cruel and unusual punishment.

The reason we have to reflect constantly on distinguishing between the reactions our alarms promote in the quest for survival versus the options that will bring more meaning to our lives is that these fork-in-the-road moments will appear many times each day. If we eat, drink, and move based on our alarms, which want us to stock up on calories, feel good, and conserve energy, we'd never leave the couch, and if we did it would only be to go to our favorite bar or restaurant for the temptation of the week.

This in no way means that we should not enjoy our temptations. We simply have to give more thought about how we live so that we can focus our minds and make choices that are healthy as well as intentionally savor special treats.

Return to the aforementioned gooey cheeseburger. You can smell it, can't you?

That's how powerful your memory center is—and you can use this power to experience the life you want. If you eat the gooey cheeseburger out of an alarm choice, you will not taste it. Your brain will have you swallowing it in three bites before you've left the parking lot. It's what you want, not what you need.

If winning the Guinness World Record for speed eating is where you're deriving meaning in your life, then absolutely gorge that burger. If this is the one time a week you splurge, roll up your sleeves and take a huge bite. But for most of us, our impulse eating is a result of not paying attention to the other options available to us.

This happens, not because we're not smart enough to know better, but because we've forgotten to step back and reorient ourselves to what's most important before we reach peak moments of fatigue, hunger, or other normal states of bodily or mental stress. When it comes to consumption, an optimal choice means having thought about what's important often enough and carefully enough so that when the time comes to make a choice we are guided by that knowledge rather than commanded to eat by our alarms.

There will always be times when something that is not the most healthy choice is the choice you make because you're truly focused on enjoyment, but that will be a choice you've made based on a partnership of your alarm ("I want that, and I have to have that, right now!") *and* your thinking center ("I know that I can trust myself to handle the pleasure without always succumbing to the cravings"). Then you have made a choice that really satisfies you, not just because it's pleasurable, but because you've used your thinking center as well as your alarm to make that decision.

## Choosing to Follow the Optimal Path

If you know your optimal emotions, values, and goals, *you actually already know your optimal choices*. Here's how it works.

Let's do a final set of SOS.

Step back. Whether you like to look, listen, or breathe, slow down. Sweep your mind like you wipe a chalkboard clean.

Now let's do a series of orientations.

First, orient yourself by choosing one *emotion* that is the most important and helpful. Feel what you want to feel right at this moment. Pull that emotion from your memory. Allow yourself to feel it. If it doesn't come easily or naturally, think of a time when you felt that optimal emotion before. It's not a problem if another emotion pops up; it's a chance to refocus on what you want to feel.

Next, continue to orient yourself by choosing *one value* that expresses the emotion that is most important. If you choose to feel happy, what is a thought that makes you happy? If you choose to feel relaxed, think of an idea that relaxes you.

Third, continue orienting by choosing *one goal* that best expresses the optimal emotion and thought that you focused on. For example, if your focal emotion is happiness and your focal thought is "I love to feel good," your optimal goal in this exercise might be, "I will build relationships that make me feel loved" or "I will do work that makes me smile."

Finally, measure your stress and personal control on a level of one to ten.

Do you see what you just did? One of the most important choices we can make is to define our identity so that our learning brains always have optimal files to access. That reduces stress and raises your ability to think clearly, the essence of personal control. You haven't just made this up—you can choose to focus on an optimal emotion, thought, or goal because you have already experienced these realities.

Using SOS to discover what you know is good and strong about yourself is a crucial missing link for most of us, and one of the best optimal choices we can make every day. Optimal choices are much easier to find and put into practice under stress when you remember the emotions, values, and goals of your optimal world. You've felt this way, lived up to your values, and reached your goals before. Optimal choices are nothing more than a continuation of those successes, and future success is always possible when we follow the optimal path.

## The Paper Clip

Here is a question as a final reminder of the hundreds of choices you have in every moment: how many different uses can you find for a paper clip?

Of course, it can keep pieces of paper neatly bound, but what about closing your bag of chips? Paper clips can be used to open certain kinds of locks, to hang a Christmas ornament from the tree, to pop a balloon after a party, and to press that tiny button to reset your son's video game. The point of thinking about all the uses of a paper clip is that you can come up with your own list.

We've given you a few to prime your thinking, come up with one more. Could you do it?

How about a second?

A third?

A hundred?

In reality, you can keep coming up with uses for the simple piece of pliable metal, as artistic as an art deco chair for your daughter's dollhouse or as practical as a money clip. But when we find ourselves in situations that cause us stress, we tend not to use our learning brains. Even sages and gurus get stuck. We have multiple options in any scenario we find ourselves in, but too often, we let the alarm drown those choices out in a flood of adrenaline and strong emotion.

*You always have choices.* When you choose the optimal path that honors both your alarm and your thinking center, you make the single most important contribution that a person can make to the world and to the lives of the people around you.

# Chapter Thirteen

# Make a Contribution

Whether you realize it or not, you already make priceless contributions to the world. Not by trying to do good deeds, but simply by resetting the alarm in your brain, and in so doing, helping other people also reset their alarms. You don't need to make yourself a better person in order to make the world a better place. You only need to remember two things: your brain has an alarm that needs your attention, and when you intentionally focus to reset your alarm, you've made a contribution.

The final skill of the FREEDOM model—*making a contribution*—is about seeing where you *already* make a positive contribution to the most important relationships, environments, and experiences of your life.

In the first chapters we taught you about your brain. Have you already taught others that they have an alarm and a thinking center and a memory center in their brains too?

If you have, it's a giant contribution. Most of us never realized that the chaos in our heads was actually just our survival brains trying to keep us safe. Most of us believe that we get stressed or melt down because there is something wrong with us, when in most situations, our alarms simply tried to make sure we didn't get hurt. Not only was there nothing wrong with us, our brains trying to keep us safe was a marvelous thing.

Most people go through their whole lives thinking something is broken in their minds, never knowing that they have the capacity to activate their brain's thinking centers with SOS, recognizing triggers, and optimizing their emotions, values, goals, and choices. Unlike you, they don't realize that they have the ability to achieve the personal control in their lives that comes from accessing not only the alarm's stress signals but also a fully optimal brain.

These are the times when a trigger sets off your alarm, and instead of freaking out at your children or spouse, coworkers or friends, you focus on what matters to you and them. Instead of reacting in a way that causes more stress, you lower everyone's stress level and elevate your personal control by focusing. How much grief will you save yourself and them because their alarms don't go off and they don't have to cope with a meltdown? How much more do you get done, simply by activating your thinking center rather than letting your alarm run your life?

As we near the end of this book, we want to show you that simply by managing your own alarm and activating your thinking center, you're already strengthening your connections with people, building stronger communities at work and where you live, and making it possible to focus on what you love to do. You don't have to change the world to make the world a better place for yourself and the people you care about. And the benefits can extend beyond your personal circle to people you don't even know.

## Your Primary Relationship

Relationships are the first and most important place to manage our own alarms. When we're an alarm-ridden mess, we affect everyone we contact that day. It is not only our opportunity, it's our responsibility to pay attention to our alarms and use our learning brains to think clearly enough to achieve a consistent level of personal control. When we don't, think of the damage we can do to the most precious people in our lives.

Let's return to the person you love most in the world.

Imagine the person's face. Imagine the person smiling, grateful to be near you. Do you think it is because you did something? The reason most of our alarms are on all the time is that we're constantly trying to earn the love, respect, and affection of the people around us. Our alarms tell us, "You better do everything right or they won't love you."

Your personal relationships, the ones you want to keep healthy and whole, are not based on the problems you solve or on constantly doing more. For the people who love you, it's your presence in this world that turns their alarms down and makes them happy to be alive. You don't have to be a rock star, a business mogul, or president. You don't have to be rich, look like a model, or do everything right. Just take care of that alarm in your brain, and you'll find that other people start to reset their alarms too. Not always, and not because you made them do it, but because being focused is just as contagious as being stressed.

Yet most of us, when we're with the people we love, try so hard, and this turns on our alarms, and often theirs too. We see them hurting, angry, sad, or in pain, and we think we have to fix it. Remember, the desire to fix is an alarm reaction. It can be helpful if what needs fixing is a real emergency, or if it is something like a button sewn on some pants or a glass of water when the person we love is thirsty. When a spouse or child or best friend struggles emotionally, however, we can't fix it. But we can give them the best kind of help possible if we reset our own alarms. We *will* have alarm reactions in response to their struggles, but all we need to do is turn down our alarms by focusing on listening to and valuing them even though their alarms are setting off our alarms.

The simplest example is at the end of the bad day. Your loved one, the one you'd do anything for, comes home grumpy, or worse, feeling beat up from school or work. It is so easy to want to make their day better. They say, "My boss is a jerk." Instead of just listening, you try to sympathize, replying, "He sure is." But instead of turning down their alarm, you just triggered it.

When your loved one comes home hurting, perhaps after losing a big deal, you try to solve the problem retroactively. You say, "Let's figure out what went wrong so it doesn't happen again." Now your loved one's alarm is going to roar even higher; she just needed to hear that she was worth loving even though things went wrong. In each case, if your response is from your alarm, you raise the alarm of the person you love even higher.

Maybe after a bad day the person you love most just needs to vent. She needs you to listen—followed by dinner, and perhaps a foot rub. In the optimal world, when people need help, they ask for it. In the real world, they often don't ask directly, however. You don't have to be a mind reader to recognize when someone else's alarm is going off.

You just need to pay attention to the way they're acting *and* to your own alarm. Don't rush. Your alarm will push you to hurry up and fix things. But if what's really important to you, if what really exercises your core values, is that your loved one knows you love and believe in her, then the best option is to show her that. But don't do this to fix something, or to "fix" her so she's instantly happy. You don't *have* to do anything.

Perhaps listening with a turned down alarm is what the person needs most. The genuine expression of warmth on your face, paying attention to her and what she is feeling, might be enough. Just hearing that she had a bad day and letting her know that she is precious even on bad days: these are the ways to keep her brain focused, and often it is the most important thing you can do for someone else.

## Family Dinner

Let's take a case study in turning down your own alarm, a situation that almost all of us deal with: family dinner. Whether at holiday time, every Sunday night, or with your spouse and children during the week (though this is becoming a lost art in our busy world), you find yourself sitting around a table with the people you love. Sometimes it's great, but then there are times when you make each other completely miserable. What do you do when the alarm sounds and you're with your family? Focus.

The food is served and everyone is enjoying the meal, until it happens: the comment. It could be Mom criticizing the way Dad's eating. It could be one sibling getting competitive with another. It could be an old family ghost of a negative past experience being brought back to life. Maybe politics or religion is your family's trigger. The reality is every family has them. These are the comments that literally steal the peace and pleasure of the meal, and once the brakes are off—and too much wine often helps speed up the meltdown—your alarm roars and you can't even taste your food.

You have the power to make a contribution in this moment. Not by saying the right thing or doing something special, but simply by noticing what's going on and not reacting. You may want to dive into the political debate, and you can; but if someone else's alarm is up, and you trigger the person further, especially if he doesn't know about his alarm, he usually won't be able to stop his reaction. He *will* escalate the debate, argument, or conflict. But it's not just his shortcomings or his problem, it's an opportunity you missed.

You can make a vital contribution, however: you can slow it down. You can step back in your mind and silently ask yourself, "What's really most important to me here?" You can smile and say, "I love how much you care about this stuff, and I really love these mashed potatoes." You can take the temperature of the room and keep managing your own alarm so you don't add more fuel to the fire. And if that doesn't work—if just being your warm self doesn't stop the train wreck of a conversation from happening—you can keep enjoying the mashed potatoes. You can keep your alarm low, and savor your food and the knowledge that your family is worth loving even when their heads are on fire. You may not choose to have long or frequent dinners with your family, but you won't end up getting burned when you do.

## Friends Who Dump You

In seventh grade, friends dump each other. Before we started dating and breaking up with romantic partners, we took out our tribal tendencies on each other. Guys and girls do it. Girls get catty, and guys ostracize the person they don't want around any more. The problem is, the tendency to dump people never ends. Women still talk about their friends and create drama that ultimately leaves someone feeling rejected. Men simply stop talking to each other and the guy who is too high maintenance doesn't get invited on next year's man trip.

In our work we've heard stories of grown men who dump their male friends because their wives asked them to. We've been told about neighbors who used to barbecue together every week and now their kids clean up after their dog and throw the bags onto each other's lawns. If you want to spend time with people, at one point or another, someone will decide you're not right for them—and getting dumped hurts. Once it's happened to you, the memory of being kicked off the island sticks with you. Every time you think it's happening again, your alarm will sound a warning signal (with a strong stress reaction) to get your attention.

That doesn't mean you have to let other people's behavior change the way you behave. Your alarm will instantly tell you one of two things: that there is something wrong with you, or something is wrong with them or the situation. If you fall into the trap of letting your alarm convince you that you're the problem, you'll start doing anything you can to remedy the situation. Your alarm will have you talking to all your mutual friends. You'll start calling, desperately trying to fix the situation. If you think they're the problem, you'll begin telling everyone else that the people who left you are crazy, that it's all their fault, or that you're just a helpless victim. Or you might end up doing anything you can to get back at them. In both cases, you'll feel worse even if you get some short-term benefits.

Why do these alarm reactions always fail sooner or later? Because they don't deal with what's really important to you. You may get to wallow in self-criticism or self-pity, or get sympathy or revenge, but you won't have exercised your core values and you won't achieve your optimal goals.

When people change, we cannot fix it. Some relationships are only meant to last a limited period of time. What we can do is know that the pain is a sign that something is wrong, and a chance for us to step back and focus until we can think clearly.

Remember the optimal emotions you've felt in your relationship. Think about what the relationship has meant to you and why you valued your friend. Then think about what you want to accomplish right now, what's really important to you, not just what you feel like doing as a reaction.

You have goals that belong to you and only you, and they can still be achieved even if the other person is not willing or able to share them with you. And you have choices that honor those core values and what you need in your life. Those options often involve other people with whom you share common goals and values, and you might choose to focus on those relationships. Rather than deny the hurt of this loss, you can affirm your life and your future.

This may seem like an extremely difficult process to take on when you're hurting badly and your alarm is taking most of your attention. But that's exactly what we all do when we recover from loss, or other kinds of stresses. We refocus on what's important, and while paying attention to the alarm's message of grief or fear or anger, we move on toward our optimal goals, guided by our core values. Focusing is not a recipe for eliminating stress or distress; it is a way to handle stress so you control how you respond to what happens in your life.

## Email, Social Media, and the Alarm

Social media has forever altered how we communicate. The good news: we can connect with people all over the world quickly. The challenge: bad news, ugly comments, miscommunication, and all the alarm flaring they can cause travel just as quickly. The reason we're bringing this up as a bridge between making a contribution in personal relationships and building community is that the growing number of ways we can connect with people is affecting our brains, and you can make sure that the positive power of social media doesn't turn into a stress-inducing nightmare.

Point one: the little devices in our pockets have a gigantic effect on our brains. Studies show that every email, text, tweet, and Facebook message generates a dopamine hit. Dopamine is the chemical that the brain produces when it is happy. We get dopamine from caffeine. We get dopamine from cocaine. A little coffee is good for us; too much and we get strung out. The same can happen with social media. A brain that is strung out is hypersensitive to triggers.

Point two: every communication can set off your alarm. At a minimum, the buzz in your pocket raises your alarm because it demands your attention. Even if just for a moment, you get adrenaline in your body. When virtual communication is not done intentionally, it is easy to be flooded by the news, conversations, and pokes it transmits.

Point three: you are in total control of your inbox. Whatever forms of virtual communication you use, you control when you use it and how you respond. You've probably already heard good advice like only check your messages a few times a day and take a break from social media for at least a few hours so you're not always on alert. But perhaps most importantly, if someone sets off your alarm with a message, you can pick up the phone and call rather than responding. If someone says something stupid on Facebook, before you ever respond, make sure your alarm is down.

The worst thing we can do in the social media world is communicate while our alarms are blaring because that snapshot of our behavior is in the public record forever. When we can be the kind of people who do an SOS every time an email, text, or message triggers us, we can also be the kind of community builder who chooses to communicate out of our optimal emotions, values, and goals, rather than reacting to what other people say when they are alarmed. You never have to press send until you're in a centered, calm place.

Your clear thinking is a contribution of incredible value you can make every day. And the message you send by resetting your alarm and focusing your thinking center is precisely what's missing in our instant communication world: speed is what the alarm craves, but accuracy and core values are what we as human beings need. A little speed can be exciting and efficient, but it's the values and goals in the message that count.

# The Guy at Your Fast-Food Joint

Here is the secret act of kindness everyone can practice that most of us never think about. Next time you go to order fast food or go to your favorite coffee shop, treat the young man at the drive-thru or the woman who pours your mocha with deep respect. We don't mean get down on your knees in reverence; we mean give the kind of graceful smile and warm greeting that you'd give an old friend.

Think about your average fast-food joint employees and their alarms. Not only are they judged by how fast they work, the work itself is repetitive, and the pay is not good. The people who eat their food want everything their way—because that's what the advertisements promise—and they don't want to pay a lot of money. They want to be treated great, and if they are eating fast food, the customers are most likely in a rush, don't have a lot of money, or are in the habit of eating fast food—all three things turn on the customers' alarms. The average fast-food worker either has numbed his alarm and goes through each day without really being present, or is grumpy because other people have been treating him poorly.

Then you walk in the door. You smile. You are polite. You're simply nice, and you say, "Thank you!"

If the person is paying attention, he will immediately smile too. The person will notice that your alarm is down and that will turn down his alarm. Most likely, he won't completely understand what you're doing. You may be so different from the other 162 people he's served that his brain won't be able to process your kindness until later. Then he will remember. He will think back on his day and you will be there, a generous person who simply treated him with respect.

This is how we can best build community from the perspective of our alarms. Our greater goals—ending homelessness, a brilliant education for every child, hunger relief for the world—start with simpler actions in our regular lives. When the world's alarm is down, optimal experiences are easier to see. When we focus on what we know we can do to turn down our alarms, others then find us the kind of people they want to work with on the global challenges we all want to see improve.

## The Angry Teammate in a Meeting

Every one of us at one point will be in a meeting—at work, in the political systems where we live, in our faith communities, and in the public square of debates, rallies, and protests—and see someone lose it.

The person gets so angry you can see the veins in her forehead and her face flushes. The whole room's alarms go off, and they should. As we talked about in the chapter on empowering emotion, anger is a sign that something is getting in the way of someone else's goals or core values. Anger, however, causes a stress response.

The first thing you have to do in a meeting where someone else gets angry is stabilize your own alarm.

Do an SOS. Orient yourself to the one thing that is important to you, what your optimal emotions, values, or goals point you toward instead of only the targets that your alarm is picking out.

Recognize your own triggers when it comes to anger. Be specific: what exactly is happening or being said or done that is triggering your alarm to send an angry message to your thinking center, demanding that you have to fix the situation or protect yourself?

Choose to see the opportunity in the high energy of the person's reaction: in that moment, people are paying attention. Focus your mind on paying attention just as carefully. But pay attention to what's really important, not to the drama or the emotional fireworks.

When you can recognize your triggers and do an SOS, your presence can help the room to come back to equilibrium.

If you're the person facilitating the meeting, when you're calm, your colleagues will be too. If you poke the angry person, you trigger her again. If you stay in a confident place where you recognize her anger and channel it into a new conversation where everyone is in control, not only do you defuse the other person's reaction, you reinforce with the group that this is a safe place to be yourself, even angry, and that there is no situation you can't handle.

Again, the key is managing your own alarm. You can't say the perfect thing to an angry person because she will either get angrier if you challenge her or even angrier if you try to soothe her—it will feel like an invalidation of what she is feeling. And you can't fight anger with anger; that only escalates into a bigger crisis. What you can do is use the FREEDOM skills that help you focus on the optimal experience in that moment, and perhaps let your actions help the other person see that it is possible to channel her alarm more intentionally.

## The Arab Spring

On December 17, 2010, Mohamed Bouazizi started a revolution that changed every country in the Middle East.

His history was not comfortable or easy. His father died when he was three, and his mother married his uncle. With his six siblings, he attended a one-room school and never graduated from high school. When his uncle's health failed, he started working at the age of ten. He applied for numerous jobs, but even his army application was rejected, so he supported his family selling produce on the streets of Sidi Bouzid, a city in the center of Tunisia and the capital of the province. Some of the reports about his life and work tell of Bouazizi, known as Basboosa to friends and family, being harassed by police since he was a child.

On December 16, he borrowed money to buy his produce to sell the next day. What we know for sure is that the next morning, the police began harassing him. Vendors had three options when facing police harassment: running and leaving their produce, paying a bribe, or getting fined. Bouazizi didn't have money that day, having invested all of his borrowed cash in his produce. Worst of all, a female municipal official confiscated his electronic weighing scales and toppled his cart. Reports differ as to whether the woman slapped him or he was beaten by her aides. Regardless, he was humiliated. He ran to the governor's office asking to be seen, just wanting his scales back so he could sell his now bruised goods.

He was not seen.

This story is interesting in terms of making a contribution: imagine where his alarm was at this point—years of abuse and trauma, incredible strain just trying to support his family, and a recent breakup with his girlfriend. What he did next absolutely looks like the reactive action of a stress response. There is no human being in the world who would not understand how Bouazizi would snap in the face of the overwhelming and continual stress that plagued him.

At 11:30, less than an hour after his fruits and vegetables rolled on the dusty ground, he stood in the middle of traffic in front of the governor's office, yelled, "How do you expect me to make a living?" covered his body in gasoline, and lit a match.

He died of his injuries. In that moment, though, was he only reacting? Or, did he intuitively manage his alarm, and choose to make a contribution for his brothers and sisters who weren't strong enough to stand up to the oppression that kept them living in poverty? We will never know his thoughts that day. What we know is that Mohamed Bouazizi sold oranges. His action started a revolution that toppled tyrannical governments. Now, in his home country, there is a postage stamp with his face on it.

## What You Love to Do

We want to make contributions in our personal relationships and in our communities because all of us need support as we build the lives we want to live. The reason: we want to do the things we love. Unfortunately, many of us are doing what we're supposed to do. Parents, teachers, and other influential adults told us what we should be, or how we should live our lives. Our alarms told us we need to do what they tell us, or we'll get in trouble. Decades later, we're following their path, not the path of learning and discovery that keeps us in the optimal world.

So let's make the greatest contribution you can in this world in addition to managing your alarm: do what you love. The idea flies in the face of many cultures around the world that value honoring our parents, sacrificing for our countries, and living for the sake of others. Those values can be the most meaningful, and we are not advocating a self-absorbed individualism that ignores the power of family and service. We just want you to fulfill those commitments and make your sacrifices because of the learning they allow, rather than the alarm-laced suffering that causes too many of us to waste precious years.

What do you love to do most?

Sports? Art? Make money? Lounge around all day? We're not judging what you love; we're emphasizing that if you're not doing it as often as you can, you're most likely living out of your alarm when you could be in your optimal world. We're not saying it is an easy or immediate path to do what is most important to you; we're simply emphasizing that you have the choice to seek that kind of life where you wake up in the morning a little more excited than you were yesterday.

That doesn't mean your alarm won't sound. It will; you want it to when you're in danger or not living your optimal life. But you control that path. You get to be the person who recognizes whether you're making a contribution by focusing on what's important to you in an optimal way or reacting to what other people want you to do.

Ask people who love what they do and they tell you they will never retire. They don't mind staying up all night working on a project. The problem for people who love what they do is to not ignore their family, friends, and community, but this is the kind of problem the alarm is made to solve in the optimal world. It will keep you safe. It will tell you when you need to rediscover an equilibrium between what you love and the people you love. But you have to pursue what you love before you can experience this kind of lovely conundrum.

# Einstein the Electrical Engineer

"Einstein the Electrical Engineer" doesn't quite have the same ring as Einstein, the brilliant mind who dissected space and time to win the Nobel Prize and change what we know about the universe forever. But it easily could have happened if Einstein hadn't done what he loved and made contributions at each stage of his life with the brain he was given. This is not the story of how you need to be like Einstein to make a contribution. This story is about a brain that never quite worked the way others thought it should. This is the true narrative of how a life with a managed alarm allows us as human beings to make the greatest contribution we possibly can.

Stories about Einstein being a poor student are false. He was always brilliant in mathematics and physics at every stage of his development. But three facts made him the kind of person who knew how to focus on what he loved rather than what others told him he should. The first: he was slow to learn to speak. His sister recalled, "Every sentence he uttered no matter how routine, he repeated to himself softly, moving his lips. He had such difficulty with language that those around him feared he would never learn." But his slowness didn't bother Einstein.

Einstein said in later life,

> *When I ask myself how it happened that I in particular discovered the relativity theory, it seemed to lie in the following circumstance. The ordinary adult never bothers his head about the problems of space and time. These are things he has thought of as a child. But I developed so slowly that I began to wonder about space and time only when I was already grown up. Consequently, I probed more deeply into the problem than an ordinary child would have.*

Whether he's exaggerating his experience or not, he let his brain focus on what he was curious about. While his trouble with language certainly raised his alarm, it also allowed him to focus on the contributions he could make. His grandparents' letters always describe him as a clever child, and he focused his brain on science.

The second fact is that not only did Einstein not fail out of school, he applied to university early. Einstein's parents wanted him to become an electrical engineer, but he hated the style of teaching at the traditional high school he attended in Germany. Instead, he applied at the age of sixteen for university. While he failed several of the tests required for entrance without his high school degree, he stood out in mathematics and physics. He tried again and the next year he passed. If he had done what his parents had wanted, he would have stayed in a school that did not excite his learning brain and perhaps toiled for the rest of his life as a solid, but uninspired electrical engineer.

Instead, the third fact about Einstein let him make his great contributions: he focused on what excited him. In one year, 1905, he published five papers, including his special theory of relativity, any one of which would have been the pinnacle of another scientist's life work.

The contributions that make us the happiest, the most confident, are not based on what others expect of us, but are found when we are trying to work on the things that excite us and that we know can be improved. Einstein knew that the work of other scientists needed to be extended. So despite opposition from the scientific community and his family, he dedicated himself to building a theory that would explain the universe. He focused on what he believed was most important, truly understanding the cosmos in all of its complexity but with a simplicity that other people could understand. That led to his great discoveries.

His ideas did not suddenly leap into his head. They were built on a lifetime of looking at the world in his unique way. Each of us is capable of the same focus. He didn't stop exploring because his university colleagues weren't applauding. He uncovered new ways of understanding the universe one equation at a time.

# I Love to Help People

Just as Einstein made a gigantic contribution by focusing each day on what he loved, you can be part of movements that change the world without having to start the next Green Peace. In the little town of Southborough, Massachusetts, in 1991, a mother and nurse who loved to feed people and a minister who noticed a need started a food pantry.

They realized that people were coming to their church occasionally looking for food, and they thought how easy it would be to put a box of food in a closet to take care of hungry folks. Notice the contribution here. Two people managed their alarms. They weren't just focused on themselves; they saw a simple opportunity and helped.

Then at a meeting of the six churches in town, they began to discuss if there were other families in need. The town of over 6,500 residents was growing, and there was likely a need greater than was showing up at the churches. The united parishes decided to take advantage of an unused closet at the back of one of the churches' halls. They filled it with shelves and made an opening by a back door so that hungry folks could come and get groceries for a week without feeling embarrassed.

By 2000, the pantry was feeding twenty families in a town that had grown to almost nine thousand people. Churches collected food. The schools did food drives. The Boy Scouts and Girl Scouts got involved. Even local retirement communities would ask people to bring food to their social events. No one did anything special. They simply picked up an extra can of soup or box of cereal. When the state started housing homeless families at a hotel in town, the pantry provided groceries and meals. When patrons of the pantry needed oil or prescription drugs they couldn't afford, the donations were used to make sure folks had what they needed.

Then in 2008, as the population of the town reached almost ten thousand residents, the economic downturn brought more hungry folks, more than forty hungry families a month. They found extra space in another empty closet, used space around the edges of a stage in the church hall, and they used a garage at one of the other churches. No one raised any alarms. The church members simply let people know about the need, and the space was created to store the food.

By 2011, the churches were feeding as many as two hundred people each week. That fall, the Scouts did their annual drive. They hung plastic bags on mailboxes around town. When people did their grocery shopping, they bought some extra noodles or tuna fish, and hung them back on their mailboxes on a Saturday morning. That fall morning, five tons of food was collected. What had started two decades earlier as a simple use of two people's optimal brains, became a movement that continues to feed hundreds of people a week.

If the nurse and the minister had decided to raise five tons of food back in 1991, it would have raised the alarms of the churches and the town. People would not have understood what was happening, and they would have fretted about where to put it. Think of the nurse and the minister if they'd tried to go big early and fix the problem immediately. Instead, they managed their alarms and the alarms of the town. They optimized their brains' ability to pay attention and help. Week by week, decade by decade, they ended hunger for an entire town.

## Secondhand Calm and Confidence

You, with your optimal brain using the messages of the alarm and the power of your learning brain, create your optimal life. You become an essential part of the universe. You are not your education, your wealth, your place in society, your job, or your material possessions. You are a unique, priceless mind, waiting to be centered and grounded in moments when the rest of the human race is stuck in alarm world. You are not the sum of your accomplishments; rather, you are the pleasure you take right now as you focus on what's most important to you.

And when you spend your conscious time in the optimal world, it will affect others. Secondhand stress has an opposite, just like Alice discovering Wonderland: secondhand confidence. When you are the kind of person who walks in the room smiling, when you know what you want to accomplish and expect to have optimal experiences, other people will want what you've got.

That confidence is what produces calm, stress-free environments. Calm breeds calm because if your brain is focused, other people's brains can focus too.

# Chapter Fourteen

# Anticipating the Pitfalls on the Way to an Optimal Life

We hope you now realize once and for all that if you want to live free from the stress that has debilitated you in the past, you can. You already had the ability, you just didn't know you had access to the solution all along. You have the choice to feel calm when you used to feel overwhelmed. You have more control than you ever thought. You, and your brain as it is today, have the ability to build the confidence you thought only belonged to movie stars, CEOs, and the greatest athletes (remember, they're struggling with the same issues you are and need to work just as hard to stay focused).

You can live in your optimal world. This is not a fairy tale or a pipe dream. This is your life. This is the life that you have the ability to affect. No one else can make the contributions you can. And, as you choose to live in your optimal world, others will try to pull you back into the world of the alarm. We're about to explore what to watch out for. The work you're doing on yourself is noteworthy, and while everyone is capable, not everyone will choose to take the steps to understand and optimize his or her brain.

## Their Alarms Are Still Sounding

The more you practice, the more the FREEDOM skills enable you to transform stress into optimal living. The more you optimize your life, the more you'll also notice that the people around you aren't focused.

The first challenge you will face as you spend more time with your alarm in control is noticing that other people are not with you; their alarms are still raging. They don't know about their brain. In the middle of a conflict or stressful situation, they will react, and not be conscious of why. When you stay in the optimal world as they melt down, they may think something is wrong with you.

You cannot turn down or reset others' alarms for them. You can absolutely slow down a conversation, show people how to orient themselves by focusing on what is really important instead of on their alarm reactions, and then check-in with yourself on whether you are feeling calmer and more in control. Another time, when their alarm levels are lower, you can even explain SOS to them, so they'll know what you're doing to stay so calm. By consciously focusing, you offer people a chance to be in the optimal world with you. They will notice, and often they will want to know what you know, so they can have an experience that is so much more pleasurable than freaking out.

But they also may turn you down, perhaps temporarily, or they may be so stuck in their alarm reactions that they can't or don't want to break the cycle of their stress responses. The alarm has its perceived pleasures. People who love the adrenaline rush, even one that comes from negative emotions like anger and conflict, may not realize that they have a pattern of living that is not compatible with yours. As you now know about the alarm and how to make it a helpful information source for creating the life you want, you can find ways to interact with alarm-ridden friends and family, coworkers and neighbors in your community, that don't stress you out. The most important way to live with people whose alarms are still on is to not let your own alarm's reactions to their stress control your choices.

But let's say the person is really struggling. Let's say she has you marked as the person who caused all the world's troubles, and she's going to hold you accountable for her misery as well as the suffering of starving children everywhere. If the person yells—and that will turn your alarm on—you do an SOS and then ask, "Can you talk calmly now or should we find another time?"

When parents, spouses, or children lose their cool because they are flooded with adrenaline, we can recognize what is happening and focus on how much we love them. We don't let them abuse us in any way, but we also understand that sometimes people melt down, and they will be grateful that we didn't respond with an equally alarm-driven reaction—and even more grateful that we are ready to reconnect once they calm down.

Because you now know that there is an optimal world, you now have an opportunity to take the old triggers that used to steal your happiness and reset your alarm so that you are not merely reacting to stress; you're thinking and acting with real personal control.

## You Will Have Bad Days

And still, some days, you will not be able to turn down or reset the alarm. Knowing about your alarm and knowing the skills to manage your stress response doesn't mean that you will always be able to feel calm and confident. If you take on challenges—like raising kids, building a career, or improving your community—you will feel your alarm raising. You will have days when bad things happen, and you just want to stay in bed.

Remember the concept of secondhand stress: if we run into a crowd of stressed-out people without doing enough SOS, we will choke on their hyperactive alarms. We will get triggered by the people, places, and experiences that unexpectedly show up and, at first, we will feel our stress response and we may not like it. We can't stop car accidents, meltdowns from friends or coworkers, or the missteps that happen to us even when we're doing our best. On our worst days, we will still, occasionally, melt down.

But not like we used to. We won't lose total control, and even if we do, we won't lose control for as long. Instead of being a victim of our circumstances and a captive of our brains, we will know that even the total meltdowns are a temporary experience. We will be able to apologize when it happens, and explain why we are struggling. We'll be able to make choices that will prevent meltdowns from happening in the same way again. We can't manage stress perfectly, and we wouldn't want to. A life without any stress is a life without energy. Remember, the alarm arouses us and keeps us focused. The key is to continually choose what you're focusing on.

## Living a Focused Life: Part I

When one of the students in Jerry's class died unexpectedly, Jerry had two problems: he was grieving the loss of a young person he cared about, and he knew every student in his class would look to him for answers. As he prepared for class that morning, he did an SOS on a picture of the young man. He pulled up the memory of him giving a speech about his grandfather's favorite one-line jokes. Most of them were terrible, but the class had never laughed so hard. Remembering the feeling filled him with a deep appreciation for who the young man was, even as he missed him.

Then he oriented to his core value as a teacher: learning. He wasn't in the class to fix the kids. His job was to listen to them, to ask questions that would help them make sense of an unexplainable situation. He didn't know why their classmate had died; he didn't have to. He simply had to give them room to be confused while at the same time assuring them that they were safe.

As the kids came into the room, many of them hugged and cried. They would be going to an assembly shortly, but Jerry had one goal: to give them a safe space to grieve. He knew that the most important learning he could offer them was that in each other there would be comfort. If he invited them to help each other, that would take away some of the weight.

At the end of the day, after constantly listening to his alarm's imperative to be the perfect teacher and make these kids happy again and choosing to focus on his optimal goal of providing a safe space, he was exhausted. It was the hardest day of his life as a teacher, and as he looked at the picture of the boy who passed away, he melted down. He cried in a way he hadn't since he was a child. He chose to keep crying until he was done.

At that moment, feeling the loss was the most important thing. Knowing how much he cared is what made him a great teacher; it's what would allow him each day to help his students learn no matter what lessons showed up in their lives.

## Living a Focused Life: Part II

Karen had been training for the hundred-mile bike race all summer. It was an optimal goal with two purposes: to get in shape and to raise money for breast cancer research, the disease that had taken her mother's life. She had been fully focused on her training. Everything was coming together, and she couldn't wait for the day of the ride and the chance to be with hundreds of other people with the same goal of racing and supporting a cause they cared about.

Three days before the race, she got sick. She could barely get out of bed. The night before the race she felt a little better, but she had a choice: Did she race and potentially have to stop? Or did she simply not try? She had every reason to stay home, and she knew her supporters would happily donate the money even if she didn't ride.

The morning of the race she still felt awful. She had drunk plenty of fluids and eaten the night before, but she didn't know how she could possibly finish the race. Her alarm told her to stay home, and to play it safe. She checked with her doctor, and he said she wasn't contagious so if she wanted to try, she should just listen to her body.

When she reached the starting line with all the other bikers, the adrenaline kicked in. Her optimal goal was to get healthy, and she'd done that. It didn't matter if she finished the race, she got herself ready to compete, and she couldn't control that she got sick. Amazingly, she still felt good after 30 miles. Instead of riding as if she was in a race, she adjusted her goal to simply ride as far as she could without hurting herself.

At mile 60, she was totally exhausted, but she connected with another group of women riding for their moms and she kept going. At mile 90, she could barely pedal. It took all her strength just to keep the bike moving forward, and she heard her alarm say loud and clear that it was time to stop.

Then she imagined her mother. She saw her mom, in her hospital bed, getting treatment, smiling. She lost her hair and the weight from her face. Cancer had taken her life, but she was still smiling.

That thought was all Karen needed. When she crossed the finish line and her husband helped her off the bike, he asked, "How did you do it? You look great."

She said, beaming, "Mom never stopped smiling, so neither will I."

## Not Everyone Will Like the New You

When you meet people who do not like the new you, the first thing to remember is that they are living out of their alarms. The key to compassion for the brokenness in our world—the brokenness that affects individuals as well as organizations, communities, and governments—is to constantly look for whether people act based on their alarms or based on their optimal brains. You have the power to do that now.

With your understanding, you can feel confidence and compassion. This is not easy and it may make others fearful or angry. But like the patient friend who loves you despite all your flaws, you don't give up on parents, siblings, and spouses just because their alarms are on. In fact, it becomes an amazing contribution to the world to provide places where, because you're paying attention, they have opportunities for their alarms to be down.

Then something unexpected may happen. With their alarms down, they notice what's happened to you. Instead of feeling threatened, they'll become curious. They'll wonder out loud and in subtle ways, "What are you doing differently? What's changed in your life? Did you lose weight?" They will ask indirectly about something their learning brains see in you, and this is when you can talk about what you know. Not like a professor or a guru. Rather, as a kind and interested friend who just wants to offer a few tidbits of wisdom you hope will be helpful.

You can give them this book. You can invite them to learn about their brains. You can tell stories about when you used to get triggered, and now, because you notice such situations, you don't. You can talk about the way you choose how you feel and think, and how it's radically different and amazing: to literally know what you want to experience and have that experience be in your control.

You can ask them to tell you about their favorite vacations, and then ask them how they feel. You'll empower their emotions, and when you give them permission to focus on optimal values, goals, and options, to make contributions instead of propagate stress, you make offerings. More often than not, they will come with you if the way in which you offer this freedom doesn't trigger their alarms.

## You May Have to Change Some Relationships

In some cases, you will decide to make changes. If the environments you live in continue to trigger your alarm, you may choose to move, leave your job, spend less time with people who used to be a regular part of your life. When relationships become truly destructive, you may need to leave entirely. Some people and places are so stuck in alarm world that they can't or won't change. We hope that they may some day, but if you think they will and the evidence continues to be that they can't, remember that secondhand stress can drain the life out of even the strongest person.

But as you leave, as you make changes, you can do it in a way that keeps you in the optimal world and gives them a chance to come with you. You don't have to be rigid or overly cruel. You don't have to shove it in their faces that they're living in alarm world. When you're desperately trying to change them, it's a sign that your own alarm is reactivating. You can gently, intentionally, do things differently. You can invite them in a clear way. With a spouse you can suggest a gentler schedule or do more of what she loves. With friends you can ask them to come for a hike rather than visit the bar. With family you can spend a day together rather than a week.

When they get angry, again, because of their alarms, you can manage yours. If you don't react, eventually they can't either. If they complain, you can immediately start talking about what you're focusing on in your life, and the pleasure it brings you—whereas in the past you might have tried to justify your choices. This may drive them crazy. Again, notice their alarm. When they openly reject you, you don't have to reject them. Bad behavior in others is based on their stress responses, not their true selves.

After too much of their bad behavior, one of your optimal choices may be to leave. No one wants to live in alarm world, and you don't have to. Or, you may be able to stay. Even though they are alarmed, you understand why they are struggling and can handle what in the past might have driven you away.

## The Optimal World

When we live in the optimal world, it will spread like laughter. Have you ever noticed how a smiling, happy person can infect a room? If their stress response is down, others, without thinking, relax as well. What if the citizens of every country knew that their alarms had value? What if they learned to manage them so that when the alarms sounded, they knew what to do? What if all of us, with intention, focused on learning? The answer to each of these questions: we would be living together in the optimal world.

It wouldn't be a perfect world. We will always be human. Our alarms are the foundation of our survival as human beings. They are still part of our biology because we still need them, even though our world has far more resources and opportunities than our ancient ancestors ever could have imagined. And the challenge of the third millennium is the evolution from the reactive beings we often are to the regulated, intentional communities we can be.

The optimal world is not a fantasy; rather, it is a choice. We can live on a planet where individuals naturally support each other. When we pay attention to our alarms, calm and confidence are likely to be the new reality of a new age. Panic and insecurity become moments when we realize that we have the power to control the way we react to the changes and challenges of being human.

We don't want our alarms to go away. We do, however, want every person to develop a brain that does not melt down unless it is necessary. We want our senses to be able to instinctively differentiate real threats from the modern sounds, sights, and feelings that need not cause our bodies to flood and our minds to become totally overwhelmed. We want our thoughts to focus on what matters, not constantly worry about having enough or consuming more.

The ancient divisions that alarmed and split communities are still with us, but they don't have to be. In the optimal world, we let ourselves be a little uncomfortable sometimes, noticing and valuing our alarms, so that we can be at peace the majority of the time. In the optimal world, every person knows that they can make a contribution in each moment and that no experience is wasted. In the optimal world, we build communities where, instead of triggering each other, we recognize each other's triggers and build organizations that take advantage of the messages the alarm sends.

We hope you will never forget that the optimal world is not a dream. It is a universal awakening to how the brain works and how to focus it on the most important needs and opportunities in our individual and communal lives. It won't take a grand marketing campaign or new world organization to build this new reality: it takes you.

Take your brain back from the alarm, optimize what your alarm and learning brain can do together, practice the skills, and one person at a time, the new way of calm, confidence, and personal control will spread across the globe.

It begins with you: every time you manage your alarm and experience freedom from stress.

# Appendix A
## Further Reading

We hope *Hijacked* has become your user's manual for understanding how stress impacts your brain, and how to regain control of your life by applying the science of mental focusing. If you'd like to learn more about the scientific and clinical foundations of the FREEDOM model and SOS, we suggest reading:

Allen, J., P. Fonagy, & A. Bateman *Mentalizing in Clinical Practice.* Washington, DC: American Psychiatric Association, 2008.

Courtois, C. A. & J. D. Ford. *Treating Complex Trauma: A Sequenced, Relationship-Based Approach.* New York: Guilford, 2012.

Courtois, C. A. & J. D. Ford, eds. *Treating Complex Traumatic Stress Disorders: An Evidence-Based Guide.* New York: Guilford, 2009.

Ford, J. D. *Posttraumatic Stress Disorder: Scientific and Professional Dimensions.* Boston: Elsevier, The Academic Press, 2009.

Ford, J. D. & C. A. Courtois, eds. *Treating Complex Traumatic Stress Disorders in Children and Adolescents: An Evidence-Based Guide.* New York: Guilford, 2013.

Herman, J. L. *Trauma and Recovery: The Aftermath of Violence—from Domestic to Political Terror.* New York: Basic Books, 1992.

If you'd like to learn more about neuroscience and the fundamentals of the brain, our favorite resources are:

Fosha, D., D. J. Siegel, & M. F. Solomon. *The Healing Power of Emotion: Affective Neuroscience, Development & Clinical Practice.* New York: Norton, 2009.

Lanius, R. A., E. Vermeten, & C. Pain, eds. *The Impact of Early Life Trauma on Health and Disease: The Hidden Epidemic.* New York: Cambridge University Press, 2010.

Perry, B. D. and Maia Szalavitz. *The Boy Who Was Raised as a Dog: And Other Stories from a Child Psychiatrist's Notebook.* New York: Basic Books, 2007.

Schore, A. N. *Affect Regulation and the Repair of the Self.* New York: Norton, 2003.

Siegel, D. J. *The Mindful Brain: Reflection and Attunement in the Cultivation of Well-Being.* New York: Norton, 2007.

Stress reduction has some classic works that we recommend. When you know how to SOS and apply the other FREEDOM skills, you'll find these techniques even more valuable.

Allen, D. *Getting Things Done: The Art of Stress-Free Productivity.* New York: Penguin Books, 2002.

Bloom, S. L. R. *Creating Sanctuary: Toward the Evolution of Sane Societies.* New York: Routledge, 1997.

Davis, Martha, Elizabeth Robbins Eshelman, and Matthew McKay. *The Relaxation and Stress Reduction Workbook.* Oakland, California: New Harbinger Publications, 2008.

Kabat-Zinn, Jon. *Full Catastrophe Living: Using the Wisdom of Your Body and Mind to Face Stress, Pain, and Illness.* New York: Delta, 1991.

Lehrer, Paul M., Robert L. Woolfolk, and Wesley E. Sime, eds. *Principles and Practice of Stress Management, Third Edition.* New York: Guilford Press, 2008.

Leyden-Rubenstein, Lori A. *The Stress Management Handbook: Strategies for Health and Inner Peace*. New Canaan, Connecticut: Keats Publishing, 1998.

Luskin, Fred and Ken Pelletier. *Stress Free for Good: 10 Scientifically Proven Life Skills for Health and Happiness*. New York: HarperCollins, 2005.

Siegel, D. J. *Mindsight: The New Science of Personal Transformation*. New York: Bantam Books, 2010.

Wehrenberg, Margaret. *The 10 Best-Ever Anxiety Management Techniques: Understanding How Your Brain Makes You Anxious and What You Can Do to Change It*. New York: W. W. Norton & Company, 2008.

# Appendix B

# A Summary of SOS

SOS is the skill that allows you to manage stress by focusing your mind on what's most important to you. This is similar to how you focus when you're trying to give your undivided attention to something that you really want to do well. Focusing always involves *choosing one thing* to pay attention to without allowing yourself to be distracted. The unique thing about doing an SOS to focus is that you choose to pay attention to the one thing *that is most important to you in your life at this moment.*

Focusing on what you value most in the present is the one sure way to turn down your stress response. We get stressed when we think or feel we *have to* solve a problem or fix a situation. Doing an SOS assures your brain's alarm that you are thinking clearly, paying attention to what you're doing, and ready to handle any challenge you face. SOS has three steps.

## Step One: Step Back

To step back is to reenter the present moment. It is to pay attention to your surroundings and to what's happening in your mind and body. Stepping back begins to reconnect the pathways between your brain's thinking center and the alarm in your brain.

Here are some common ways to step back:

- Sweep your mind clear of all thoughts, like erasing a chalk board
- Slow down the pace of your mental and physical activity
- Close your eyes and listen
- Look at something beautiful
- Count to ten
- Take three intentional breaths

## Step Two: Orient

To orient is to focus your mind entirely on one thought. That thought—an image, a sensory experience, an emotion, a value, or a goal—is whatever *at this moment* is *most important to you in your life*. Focusing on *just one thought* activates your thinking center, the brain's frontal lobes, and this turns down your brain's alarm.

Some common examples of orienting are:

- A parent enjoying watching her child as she plays
- A painter concentrating on the feel of the brush in his hand
- A golfer thinking only about his next shot
- A leader pausing in her work to appreciate her team
- A teacher re-reading a student's eloquent sentence
- A diner savoring the taste of delicious food
- A busy executive who stops to visualize a favorite vacation place
- A singer who concentrates on the feeling of joy as she sings
- An airline pilot who visualizes a safe landing as he brings the plane in
- You thinking about your very favorite place or person

What you orient yourself to is very specific, and it is about what is good and safe in your life. When you orient you aren't trying to fix anything or solve any problems, you appreciate what you have in your life that gives you a sense of purpose and confidence.

## Step Three: Self-Check

To self-check is to measure the level of stress you're feeling and your level of personal control on scales of 1–10. Here are two simple, practical scales you can use:

### *Stress Level*

| No stress, best you've ever felt | | | | Definite but manageable stress | | | Worst stress ever | | |
|---|---|---|---|---|---|---|---|---|---|
| 1 | 2 | 3 | 4 | 5 | 6 | 7 | 8 | 9 | 10 |

Stress is not good or bad; it is a physical reaction from your body and brain that is intended to help you be safe. So even though a 10 is the highest level of stress you've ever felt, high levels of stress aren't something you can't handle. Your brain, recognizing you're facing a serious situation, just needs to gear up to handle the challenge.

A "1" or "2" stress level is like what you feel when you've just woken up well rested from a great night's sleep—feeling calm, pleasantly energized, and refreshed.

### *Personal Control Level*

| Low Control | | | | Some Personal Control | | | High Personal Control | | |
|---|---|---|---|---|---|---|---|---|---|
| Reacting without thinking | | | | Beginning to think before reacting | | | Thinking very clearly | | |
| 1 | 2 | 3 | 4 | 5 | 6 | 7 | 8 | 9 | 10 |

Personal control is your ability to think clearly. A high level of personal control such as a "9" or "10" is when you can think completely clearly without being distracted by any worry, anger, fear, or doubt from your brain's alarm. A "1" is when you're feeling confused, or pressured, or find yourself reacting without thinking when you feel stressed.

Instead of simply reacting based on the alarm's commands, doing the stress and control ratings jump starts your brain's thinking and memory centers. If our initial stepping back and orienting don't turn down stress, self-checking stress and personal control activates the learning brain, helping us begin to feel better and think more clearly.

# Appendix C

# A Summary of the FREEDOM Skills

**F**ocus. To focus is to maximize your personal effectiveness by doing an SOS both in times of stress and, most importantly, when you're not stressed. When you practice focusing at times when you're not alarmed, this prepares you to be able to turn down your brain's alarm (and regain personal control) more quickly when you face stressful situations. Focusing is not only about managing stress, but also about being personally effective and making the most of your life.

**Recognize Triggers.** To recognize triggers is the act of engaging the thinking center so you are fully aware of exactly what is turning on your alarm at a given moment. When you intentionally pay attention to what's triggering you, you're better able to think clearly about how to handle it. This builds a partnership between your alarm and thinking center.

**Empower Emotions.** To empower emotions is the act of listening to your alarm and the reactive emotions it causes you to feel. Empowering emotions also includes activating the memory center to recall emotions that represent how you feel at your very best. When you recall an optimal emotion from your past, you enable your brain to identify the alarm emotion and then reorient to the emotion you want to feel right now. By paying attention to both your alarm's reactive emotions and your optimal emotions, you forge an even stronger partnership between your alarm and thinking center. That partnership is the missing key to turning down the alarm and effectively managing stress.

**Exercise Your Core Values.** To exercise your core values, you begin by paying attention to the thoughts that your alarm communicates as reactions to immediate stressors. This enables your thinking center to evaluate those thoughts before simply reacting. Then your thinking center can create a new value or retrieve a thought from your memory center that expresses what is most important to you in your life.

**Determine Optimal Goals.** To determine your optimal goals is to identify both the goals that your alarm is pushing you toward and the goals that reflect your core values. When you respect your alarm's goals and expand them by activating your thinking center to include your core goals, you've enhanced your personal control. This further turns down and resets your alarm.

**Optimize Your Choices.** To optimize your choices is to remember in every moment that you have a choice between two important options. The first option is to follow the commands of your alarm to solve a problem or get away from danger. The second option is to follow the optimal goals that are grounded in your core values, by acting based on what's most important to you. When you consider both options before you act, you have completed the partnership between your thinking center and your alarm. That win-win choice is the single most effective way to turn down and reset your alarm, and to achieve true personal control.

**Make a Contribution.** Each time you focus your mind and make choices based on what is most important to you as well as on the input from your alarm, you have made the world a better place. Instead of letting your alarm's reactions to stress totally determine the way you live, you use those stress reactions as a reminder to pay attention to what really matters in your life. You can't singlehandedly make this an optimal world, but when you turn down the alarm in your own brain you're making a big contribution to everyone in the world. Turning down your alarm helps everyone whose life you touch to turn down their alarms as well.

# Acknowledgments

Julian is very grateful to the clients, mentors, colleagues, students, friends, and family members who have enriched his professional and personal life by teaching him how to transform stress into a life worth living. Above all, to his parents, his daughters, sons-in-law, and grandchildren, and his wife and partner professionally and in life, Judy.

Jon is grateful to Bob Bachelder, Dave Pezzino, and Jen Wortmann as well as the leaders and staff at Pilgrim and the Healthy Living Group for their support and wisdom.

We sincerely thank our agent, Giles Anderson, for making *Hijacked* possible, and our editor, Shana Drehs, for enabling us to put this new way of thinking and being into words.

# About the Authors

Dr. Julian Ford is a clinical psychologist and Professor of Psychiatry at the University of Connecticut and a researcher, clinician, and teacher in the field of traumatic stress and psychotherapy. He has coedited or coauthored seven books for professionals in practice and in training on the translation of psychological and neurobiological science into effective therapies for traumatic stress and related psychosocial disorders. He lives with his wife in Farmington, Connecticut.

Jon Wortmann is a non-profit leader and leadership coach and trainer. He is the coauthor of two books, *Mastering Communication at Work* and The *Three Commitments of Leadership*, and has worked with educational, start-up, and Fortune 500 corporations. He lives with his wife in Ellington, Connecticut.